HONORABLE INFLUENCE

A CHRISTIAN'S GUIDE TO FAITHFUL MARKETING

DAVID HAGENBUCH

foreword by PETER GREER

ALDERSGATE
PRESS

In *Honorable Influence*, David Hagenbuch provides a valuable "How To" guide for applying the key tenets of Christianity to make the honorable practice of marketing even more honorable.

Keith Reinhard
Chairman Emeritus
DDB Worldwide

• • •

In a world that uses analytics and Big Data to justify low brow campaigns to achieve a targeted goal, David has opened the door of accountability for those of us who are Christian practitioners in the field of Sales and Marketing.

He has refined our definition of Value, in relationship to the exchanges in our commerce, that we proliferate in society.

David's challenge to Sales and Marketing professionals is to apply the Golden Rule to your own heart before you ask others for theirs.

In writing *Honorable Influence*, David has helped Christian Sales and Marketing professionals to realize that we indeed have a voice and are charged with being accountable to a higher calling when we use it.

I can imagine the prophet Daniel writing a similar book based on the II Corinthians 5:20 and following a similar path of *Honorable Influence* for life.

> We are therefore Christ's ambassadors, as though God were making his appeal through us. We implore you on Christ's behalf "Be reconciled to God." — II Corinthians 5:20

Kevin Smith
Director of New Business Development
J. Walter Thompson Worldwide

HONORABLE INFLUENCE
By David Hagenbuch

Copyright © 2016 David Hagenbuch

ALDERSGATE **PRESS**
THE PUBLICATIONS ARM OF

HolinessandUnity.org

In Collaboration with

LAMP POST inc.
www.lamppostpublishers.com
Spring Valley, CA

Printed in the United States of America

Soft Cover ISBN 13:   978-1-60039-308-2
ebook ISBN-13:   978-1-60039-980-0

Library of Congress Control Number: 2016946569

To my families, Hagenbuch and Shulgach,
for your honorable influence in my life

CONTENTS

FOREWORD

by Peter K. Greer

Peter is the President and CEO of HOPE International, a global Christ-centered microenterprise development organization serving throughout Africa, Asia, Latin America, and Eastern Europe. He is also the author of several books including *The Poor Will Be Glad* (with Phil Smith, 2009), *The Spiritual Danger of Doing Good* (with Anna Haggard, 2013), and *Mission Drift* (with Chris Horst).

Imagine a morning when everything is going wrong. You wake up with the flu, complete with the symptoms we all know and dread—burning fever, splitting headache, runny nose, and an overwhelming sense of exhaustion. Given that you can barely rise to a sitting position, you certainly don't have the energy to get your kids off to school, so they're playing on the floor in yesterday's pajamas while you try to rest. You haven't combed your hair. You have dark bags under your blood-shot eyes.

It's at this moment that a film crew bursts into your home and begins taking shots of you and your family. You try to explain that it's most certainly *not a good time*, but they assure you they won't be long. After fifteen minutes of bright camera flashes, the crew members vanish as suddenly as they appeared.

As degrading as that experience might sound, that's not the end of it. To your shock and horror, several weeks later you see these photos of you and your family featured in glossy brochures and sprinkled throughout internet ads.

Most degrading of all, though, is the message behind these materials: Give money to help desperate families like this one. Does this scenario seem far-fetched? It's actually not as unrealistic as you might imagine.

Beginning as far back as the 1890s, people discovered that dramatic images of human need served as an effective tool in raising money for a variety of causes (Parisi, 2015). The greater the need suggested by the image, they reasoned, the greater the response. Taking this ends-justify-the-means free license, marketers have found people on their worst days, in the worst conditions. In the name of advocacy, they capture these compromising and even humiliating moments and distribute them for all to see, without any attempt to secure the permission of the subjects. Faith-based organizations are not exempt from this practice and have resorted to sharing images and stories in a way that exploits the very people they serve.

Several years ago, I was convicted of this personally as I saw images on the screen behind me during a presentation which I know did not honor the people we were serving. The result might have been a few donations, but it came at too high a cost. There is no financial justification to eroding the dignity of individuals created in God's image.

I believe the stories that we tell and the way we market our mission matters—*especially* when we claim to follow Jesus. For those who follow Christ, it's not enough to simply have influence; we must seek to have *honorable* influence. This conviction comprises the centerpiece of David Hagenbuch's work in marketing, as well as the message of this groundbreaking book. Drawing on a rich array of scriptural insight, personal experiences, and practical application, David identifies the "seven deadly sins" of influence to reveal how poor practices undermine our professional credibility as well as our faith witness.

But even as he addresses these "sins," David wisely avoids the temptation to portray marketing as an entirely negative or unwholesome discipline. Rather, he makes the case that marketing is a vital component of a socially and economically thriving society. It helps maximize the value of exchange. It helps businesses thrive and create jobs so that families and communities are strengthened.

Beyond the societal value of marketing, David boldly contends that it's also a high calling and vocation. We need marketing professionals who take their faith seriously, recognizing the call to go beyond the financial bottom line. David makes this argument—and he models it himself.

At its core, *Honorable Influence* charts a third way, demonstrating how marketing done with integrity positively impacts everyone involved, from producers to consumers to marketers. The principles in this book have broad application in for-profit and nonprofit, faith-based and secular settings. The missions of our organizations are too important to miss out on the opportunity to re-explore the marketing profession and to pursue influence—honorably.

INTRODUCTION

Who are the people who have been most influential in your life? Maybe they're your parents, grandparents, or other relatives. Or perhaps some special teachers, coaches, or pastors come to mind. There's another group of people you probably didn't consider who have influenced you ceaselessly since your earliest years and continue to do so today. In fact, over your lifetime these people might impact you more than any other group. Who are they? Marketers. Some have estimated that during the course of a day the average American is exposed to 5,000 marketing messages (Smith, 2016). This figure is probably high, but even if the actual number is a couple of thousands or hundreds (Johnson, 2014), that's a tremendous amount of commercial content crossing your senses. Consequently, it's doubtful that any business discipline directly touches as many lives as marketing does. In fact, there are relatively few societal institutions that have as frequent and far-reaching an impact on the general populace as does marketing (Matear & Dacin, 2010; Sheth & Sisodia, 2005).

What do people make of marketing's ubiquitous and largely unavoidable influence? Many don't like it—at least that's what Gallup research results seem to suggest. Nearly every year since 1977, Gallup has conducted a poll asking respondents to "rate the honesty and ethical standards" of individuals in various fields. In the latest poll nurses, medical doctors, and pharmacists garnered the top three spots, followed by high school teachers and police officers. At the very bottom of the list were advertising practitioners, car salespeople, members of Congress, telemarketers, and lobbyists (Saad, 2015). It's not surprising to see marketing professions occupy three of the bottom five positions—to hear people denounce the discipline, even in casual conversation, is not unusual. Although marketing doesn't deserve much of the criticism it receives, there is no denying that the field experiences its fair share of moral lapses, which has led to poor impressions of the discipline for many decades. For example, over nearly forty years of polling, Gallup respondents have consistently ranked advertisers near the bottom of the list in terms of honesty and ethical standards. Almost every year only 10-12% of respondents have rated advertising practitioners high or very high on morality, while 30-40% or more consistently rate the profession's ethics low or very low (Honesty/Ethics, 2014).

Everyone has a stake in the game, not just the marketers.

If you're a marketer, these results should shake you up if not rock your world! You may be thinking, "Besides those entrenched in organized crime, who wants to be employed in a field associated with such disrepute?" If you're a *Christian* marketer, the Gallup results should cause you to do some serious soul-searching: "Can my marketing career really be part of a kingdom calling? God has put me in a position of influence, but what kind of influence am I having?" If you're *not* a marketer *or* a Christian you should be asking yourself, "Why am I even reading this book?"—but in all seriousness, your broader interest best reflects this book's ultimate aim, which is much bigger than just restoring the reputation of an oft-disparaged discipline.

The purpose of *Honorable Influence* is to help move the needle on marketing morality and ensure that the field's impact is more consistently positive. Sure, it would be nice to see marketing occupations move up the ranks in Gallup polls, but that change is the lowest priority. More importantly, our world needs more marketers who take very seriously the persuasive power they hold and who seek to use it in ways that genuinely benefit others, especially given the far-reaching impact the discipline has on individuals, organizations, and institutions, including the Church. Everyone has a stake in the game, not just the marketers.

Of course, for Christians there's an all-important stakeholder, God, who asks that we do everything "in the name of the Lord Jesus" (Colossians 3:17, NIV). That everything includes marketing. Yes, it's very important that marketing's influence honors people, but what God thinks matters more than Gallup poll results, which of course is a huge understatement. If Christian marketers are not influencing honorably, they're failing to fulfill their Christian calling, and they're missing a great opportunity to make a very unique kingdom impact. Fortunately, God's Word provides the keys to influencing honorably. Even though a Bible concordance search for "marketing" produces no hits, scripture is replete with timeless principles and instances of proper influence. It's also helpful that over millennia many, many marketers have practiced the tenets of their field faithfully, providing countless examples of marketing done right. *Honorable Influence* is about celebrating and encouraging such successful influence.

So, whether you're reading this book as a person who enacts marketing influence, or you're someone whom that influence affects, I congratulate you for recognizing the far-reaching importance of this unique topic. I also welcome you to what I believe you'll find to be an interesting and enlightening inquiry. Let's begin the journey into *Honorable Influence*.

PART 1:

A PROPER CONTEXT

Have you ever been part of a conversation when somehow the topic changes, unbeknownst to you? Suddenly you're listening to people make comments that don't make much sense or may even seem irreverent. Such situations are good reminders that we're always better off hearing and interpreting information in the appropriate context. Such is the goal of this book's first two chapters.

Chapter One, "You Work in Marketing?" presents the question that many Christian marketers have heard multiple times, usually expressed with a measure of disbelief. Whether or not you work in marketing, it's important to recognize the cynicism that many have about the field. Perhaps Christian marketers feel this distrust more keenly than others.

The main goal of Chapter Two, "Understanding Marketing Influence," is to introduce and define the book's two central concepts: marketing and influence. Given that many people have a narrow view of the discipline, it's important to provide a succinct yet complete picture of all that *marketing* entails, which will later shape the discussion of specific ethical issues. Likewise, readers need a working definition of *influence*, particularly one that distinguishes it from related concepts like encouragement and persuasion.

With this context in place, we will then be ready to tackle the rest of this book's tumultuous topics.

Chapter 1
YOU WORK IN MARKETING?

The way that I approach my entire racing career is to do it right.
—Willy T. Ribbs

Sometimes I wonder what it would be like to get a *really* positive re-sponse from someone when I tell them what I do for a living. You know how it goes. You're at a gathering, meeting new people. You find yourself talking with a person you've never met before. Pretty soon you're asking about each other's work.

> *Me:* "So, what do you do?"
> *Him:* "I'm an orthopedic surgeon."
> *Me:* "Wow, that's great. It must be very satisfying to help people overcome physical challenges."
> *Him:* "Yes it is."
> *Long pause.*
> *Him:* "And, what do you do?"
> *Me:* "I teach at a Christian College."
> *Him:* [cautiously interested] "That's nice. What do you teach?"
> *Me:* "Business courses; mainly marketing."
> *Him:* [surprised and nearly speechless] "Oh."

In terms of responses to my career field, "Oh" is about as positive as they come. I'm not complaining, though. The reactions can be worse. Sometimes my discipline is implicitly blamed for American materialism or unseemly television commercials. Others can't resist the temptation for some good-natured ribbing, like a colleague of mine who quipped, "You teach Marketing Principles? Isn't that an oxymoron?" I really don't mind these responses; they come with the territory. I love my field and understand its social and economic value, even if not everyone does. Plus, I remind myself that I probably get off easy compared to my friends in law and politics.

More than people's general reaction to marketing, what intrigues me most is the frequent disbelief that someone can actually be a Christian *and* work in marketing. Few individuals come right out and verbalize their skepticism, but they don't have to. I can see it in their faces and infer it from their questions and comments. They're wondering, "How is it possible for him to follow Christ and do what marketers do?" This perceived disconnect often stems from a narrow view of what marketing is and/or from some bad consumer experiences with certain organizations that approached marketing improperly. The primary professional affiliation for marketers, The American Marketing Association (AMA), defines marketing as "the activity, set of institutions, and processes for creating, communicating, delivering, and exchanging offerings that have value for customers, clients, partners, and society at large" (About AMA, 2013). I will explain more about what marketing is and how it involves influence in Chapter Two, but suffice it here to say that many people hold a distorted view of the discipline.

> *What intrigues me most is the frequent disbelief that someone can actually be a Christian and work in marketing.*

On the spiritual side, these misperceptions are compounded by a lack of recognition of many positive scriptural references to marketing. True, the Bible never uses the word *marketing*, but it still offers commentary on the discipline. One of my favorite passages in the Bible is the epilogue to Proverbs, the second part of Chapter 31, which describes the *Wife of Noble Character*. While I enjoy the entire passage, I'm particularly pleased to hear God commend a businessperson who engages in various types of commerce and who "sees that her trading is profitable" (Proverbs 31:18). There's tremendous validation of business here. However, the *coup de gras* involves the implications of Jesus being a carpenter, which was his job before his years of public ministry (Mark 6:3). It stands to reason that people who participated in trades like carpentry would have sold or traded their wares, not kept all of them for their own use. Consequently, Jesus must have been involved in marketing. Of course, Jesus also was without sin, which suggests that there is nothing inherently sinful about the discipline.

Despite this and other scriptural validation, it's often been my experience that people are dubious of the notion that marketers can honor God while attempting to influence people—a central function of the discipline. As you know by now, the premise of this book is just the opposite: It is quite possible to be a faithful follower and an effective marketer. During more than 25 years of working in marketing and teaching in the discipline, I've given considerable thought to what it means to be a Christian in marketing. In fact, in an article I wrote a several years ago, "Marketing as a Christian Vocation" (Hagenbuch, 2008), I wrestled with and, I believe, supported the notion that marketing is fundamentally compatible with Christianity. I share this article routinely with my students, who tend to gain confidence from it, finding confirmation of their major and career

> *Jesus must have been involved in marketing.*

choice. I encourage you to read the "Vocation" article too, which can be found in this book's appendix. In fact, you may want to read the article before you read this book's other chapters.

The "Vocation" article is largely a theoretical piece, analyzing marketing's key tenets in the abstract. Because it's hard to move forward into more concrete discussions without embracing a proper philosophy of marketing, this book will also offer some brief treatment of the discipline's basic nature and purpose. Unlike the article, however, this book is intended to be more of a practical guide to "faithful" marketing. While it's helpful to identify the foundational compatibility between

Christianity and marketing, it's important that the discussion not end there. Christians working in marketing, and those who share similar values, deserve some practical guidelines for their daily work.

The challenge with this charge is that marketing is a vast and diverse field. All types of organizations from Fortune 100 global companies to small church congregations utilize marketing concepts. Similarly, people who practice marketing include CEOs, salespeople, graphic artists, researchers, brand managers, website developers, creative directors, content writers, and customer service personnel. This breadth and depth makes it difficult to offer a comprehensive set of prescriptions for the field, i.e., "this is the way to do A, B, and C." Given this tremendous divergence, it makes most sense to identify what *not* to do, or to elucidate the common *influence pitfalls* that marketers should avoid.

This approach of offering guidance through negative injunctions is not uncommon. For instance, when governments attempt to frame the parameters for good citizenship they generally don't detail every *acceptable* civic practice. Instead, they usually compose lists of *inappropriate* behaviors. All other actions, by extension, are acceptable. Similarly, when God described to Adam His policy on eating the fruit of the Garden, He didn't delineate tree by tree every type of edible fruit; rather, he pointed to one tree and said don't eat from that one; all the others are okay (Genesis 2:15-17).

People are dubious of the notion that marketers can honor God while attempting to influence people.

This book follows the same protocol by identifying for marketers the forms of influence they should avoid. Still, this approach is not without challenge. Even a new critic of the field might think: "The practice of marketing is full of questionable activities; good luck describing all of them." What the casual observer may not realize, however, are the commonalities among many of these practices. For instance, a television commercial shows a cheeseburger that looks much bigger and juicer than any burger you could ever buy at the fast-food chain. And, a salesperson tells a prospect who's working against a tight timeframe that most orders ship within two weeks, not revealing that a labor strike at the factory appears imminent. On the surface these two unscrupulous actions seem unrelated. Closer analysis, however, reveals that both rely on deception to entice consumers to choose something they might otherwise reject.

Such is the case with most of the unscrupulous activities performed under the auspices of proper marketing. While there are hundreds of different dishonest actions that misguided individuals may commit, most, if not all, of these actions are related in that they violate one of a handful of moral/biblical principles. In fact, based on my work experience in marketing, as well as over fifteen years teaching marketing and ethics courses, I have identified seven unique categories of immoral behavior, which I call the "Seven Sins of Influence." Here are the Seven Sins, with a brief definition of each:

1. *Deception*: leading another to believe an untruth
2. *Coercion*: pressuring people to do something against their will
3. *Manipulation*: scheming to achieve an outcome that otherwise would not be chosen
4. *Denigration*: cheapening the inherent worth of people or things
5. *Intrusion*: entering another person's physical or mental space without the other's complete welcome
6. *Encouraging Overindulgence*: prompting excess beyond what's beneficial for individuals physically, emotionally, financially, or otherwise
7. *Neglect*: not offering the influence that is expected from a competent professional in a given field

It is my contention that every instance of unethical influence can be categorized within one of these seven areas. You might be thinking, "Well that's nice, but what's the point?" In other words: *What are the benefits of such a classification system?* The value, first and foremost, is greater potential for ethical marketing behavior—an outcome that will benefit everyone, whether inside or outside the field. Again, given the discipline's broad array of functions and numerous areas of applications, it's a daunting task for marketers to have a well-reasoned view on every potential ethical issue in the field. The seven categories, therefore, provide marketers with a framework for evaluating the morality of actions involving influence, one of the discipline's primary functions, through seven straight-forward questions: Is the action deceptive; is it coercive; is it manipulative . . . ?

As such, individuals in any organization, from for-profit companies to churches, can apply the system to any marketing strategy or tactic. For example: Is the method of conducting the survey intrusive? Does the use of sexuality in the magazine ad denigrate women? Does discontinuing production of replacement parts for last year's model constitute manipulation? Is the approach for soliciting gifts to the church's building campaign coercive? Of course, questions like these still may not be easy to answer, but individually and collectively they represent a vast improvement over the less rigorous alternatives, such as: "We've always done it that way," or "It seems okay to me," or "This approach will make the most money."

More specifically, Christians working in marketing might find this book to be a helpful companion to Brown and Wiese's (2014) *Work That Matters*, which adeptly explains why all work is important to God and should be understood as worship. Brown and Wiese's discussion also extends well beyond the "why" question, as the authors illuminate several practical ways in which Christians can ensure that their work is purposeful service to God and others. In a way, then, *Honorable Influence* picks up where Brown and Wiese leave off by unpacking the morally complex discipline of marketing and describing with specificity how believers can work in the field for the glory of God.

This book's framework for analysis should also directly benefit consumers. Sometimes as consumers we don't readily recognize when we're being taken advantage of in an exchange. Or, we have a feeling that something's amiss, but we can't articulate exactly why. The same sort of uncertainty, by the way, crops up in other areas of our lives, too, involving things such as our health, finances, and relationships. In any case, the Seven Sins paradigm might help consumers to more easily identify abuses of marketing influence and to hold unscrupulous practitioners accountable.

Seven subsequent chapters of this book are dedicated to an in-depth examination of each of the Seven Sins, explaining and elucidating each category. Every individual analysis will include an exploration of scripture, identifying Bible passages that treat the behavior in question. The focus will then shift to the field of marketing, considering examples both of activities that violate underlying moral principles and actions that uphold them. As suggested above, these examples will be taken from various parts of the marketing process. Before embarking on this exploration, however, it is important to establish a context for the discussion that will follow, which means describing the nature and purpose of both marketing and influence. These objectives are the task of the next chapter.

> *Activities that lead consumers into exchanges that do not benefit them don't deserve to be called marketing.*

Finally, the older I get, the more I realize the value of expectation management—letting people know upfront where things are headed, or how they'll be handled. So, in that spirit, allow me to make the following disclosure. In case you haven't already gotten this impression, this book does not offer a wholesale indictment of marketing, like many today are inclined to provide. So, if you're expecting someone to rail against the discipline, you'll be disappointed. At the same time, this book also does not attempt to present a sterilized version of a field that can do no wrong. Even though my job title includes the word *marketing*, I'm a sharp critic of marketing practices that stray from the discipline's central philosophy and core values. Activities that lead consumers into exchanges that do not benefit them don't deserve to be called marketing. Ultimately, however, I'm one of the field's biggest fans and firmly believe that marketing practiced with integrity holds uniquely great potential for honoring all stakeholders: consumers, marketers, society, and God.

Reflection Questions – Working in Marketing

1. Does marketing deserve its negative reputation? Why or why not?

2. What biblical support is there for marketing?

3. Does the Bible speak against marketing, and if so, how?

4. How is it best to respond to people who disparage your discipline?

5. How is marketing part of your life?

Chapter 2
UNDERSTANDING MARKETING AND INFLUENCE

Blessed is the influence of one true, loving human soul on another.

—George Eliot

Most people like to receive compliments from others, and I'm certainly no exception. At one family gathering my mother-in-law approached me and proceeded to boost my ego.

> *Mama:* "I'm so proud of you. You're smart . . . you teach college . . . you're a doctor . . . "
> *Me:* [I'm trying to think of ways to disagree, but her argument is so convincing.]
> *Mama:* "I just have one question."
> *Me:* "Yes, Mama, what is it?"
> *Mama:* "What is marketing?"
> *Me:* [My bubble bursts, but I still appreciate her well-intended compliments.]

The great thing about parents is that they love you unconditionally, even if they don't understand exactly what you do. In all fairness to my mother-in-law, though, she's in good company when it comes to having a less-than-complete picture of marketing. The discipline tends to be one that everybody knows of, but few completely understand. Perhaps other marketers and I need to do a better job marketing *marketing*. So, for Mama's benefit, and for everyone else who would like a primer, here comes a concise overview of the discipline. In addition, this chapter describes an intimately related concept that is the book's other main construct—*influence*. Both of these discussions provide important context for later treatment of the *Seven Sins*.

What is Marketing?

In the first chapter I shared the AMA's definition of marketing, which is very good. I like to explain marketing with a description that's consistent with the AMA's definition but is more concise and perhaps easier to remember: *marketing is the science that seeks to facilitate mutually beneficial exchange*. Some believe that marketing is pure art, and I agree that marketing benefits greatly from creative input. It's important to note, however, that marketing *is* a science; it has the key characteristics of a science, and it is amendable to research via scientific method (Hunt, 2002). So, the process of implementing effective marketing is largely driven by objective and systematic criteria, not simply a subjective sense of what feels right, looks good, or sounds nice.

Now onto the meat of the definition: To *facilitate* means to ease or enable, which is not difficult to understand, but what is *mutually beneficial exchange*? First, *exchange* occurs when people or organizations give up something they own in order to acquire something they want more. Trade and barter are good synonyms for exchange; although, these terms may unnecessarily imply goods alone. Exchange often involves currency, of course. Likewise, exchange is not limited to physical goods; it can involve intangibles like services and ideas (Lamb, Hair, & McDaniel, 2010).

The final part of the definition is the critical qualifier that many people don't associate with marketing: *mutually beneficial*. True marketing is designed to meet the needs of *both* buyers and sellers. Some people hold a rather cynical view of marketing and exchange. They think that for one party to benefit, the other has to lose. There's little economic basis for this belief; rather, the reality is that people and organizations engage in mutually beneficial exchange all the time, in both commercial and non-commercial contexts. Consider a marriage: a husband and wife each benefit from sharing their time, energy, and

> *True marketing is designed to meet the needs of <u>both</u> buyers and sellers.*

affection with their spouse. Or, take employment: Employers profit from the productivity of their employees, and employees gain from things such as pay and job satisfaction.

There's no reason to believe that exchanges must be limited to one "winner." As such, the goal of marketing is to produce win-win, or "mutually beneficial," outcomes. This purpose is represented in the simple diagram below (Figure 1). One circle represents the organization's, or marketer's, goals. The other represents the needs of consumers. Marketing strives to maximize the overlap of these two circles—the intersection that symbolizes *mutually beneficial exchange (MBE)*.

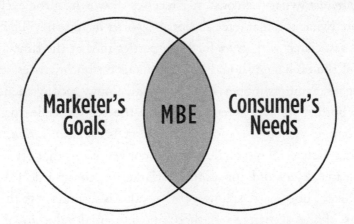

FIGURE 1. MARKETING'S GOAL OF MUTUALLY BENEFICIAL EXCHANGE (MBE).

For a marketing exchange to be mutually beneficial there must be a freely chosen and fair transfer of value. In a simple two-party exchange, both parties enter into the transaction voluntarily, with *informed consent*, i.e., they're fully aware of *what* they're doing and they *want* to do it (Informed Consent Law, 2015). The reason the parties want to exchange is that each values the other party's possession more than their own. For consumers, that something is often a product, e.g., a loaf of bread, a pair of shoes, a cellphone, etc. The consumer has money, but he can't eat it, wear it, or use it to communicate, so he is glad to give up $3, $60, or $600 for things that will provide him with greater utility than does the money in his pocket. On the other side of the exchange, the cellphone maker has thousands more phones than it needs, so it wants to give up phones in return for money, which it needs to pay employees, provide returns to shareholders, etc.

> The goal of marketing is to produce win-win, or "mutually beneficial," outcomes.

For several decades, marketers have used the *marketing mix* and the iconic "Four Ps" (product, price, place, and promotion) to describe the key elements in an exchange (Magrath, 1986). Although each of the Ps signifies value in some sense, the ones that most directly represent value are *product* (what the consumer receives of worth in the exchange) and *price* (what the marketer accepts of worth in return). There also is value associated with *place* for both parties in that the time and location of the exchange should be convenient for both parties. As the saying goes, "time is money," and as we all know, inconvenience can cost us both. *Promotion* represents how the consumer learns about the exchange; although a more fitting term is *communication*, which more accurately symbolizes the two-way conversations that often occur between marketers and consumers. Marketing communication does hold value for both parties; however that value is secondary to the other elements of the exchange. If there's no potential value in product, price, and place, there's not much point in communicating.

So, a mutually beneficial marketing exchange involves a freely chosen and fair transfer of value that stems mainly from the configuration of product, price, and place. How do we know, however, that the parties both received fair value? If each entered into the exchange with informed consent and neither had regrets afterward, it was a mutually beneficial exchange.

Marketing Influence

Generally speaking, it's the job of marketers to initiate exchanges. Consumers don't typically think, "I have some money; I need to find something to spend it on." And, even when they recognize their unmet needs, it can be difficult for them to find specific possibilities for satisfying those needs unless there's some initiative on the other side, from the marketers. It's up to marketers, therefore, to let consumers know that the potential for exchange exists. This notification represents a key component of *marketing influence*. More generally, *influence* is what makes most exchanges possible and profitable for both parties. Influence is the water that primes the pump to start the exchange and the grease between the wheels that keeps the process moving. Although consumers increasingly influence exchanges too, it is foremost the marketer's responsibility to do so.

Given that influence is such a vital component of marketing, it's important to define the term. Likewise, because the remainder of this book seeks to distinguish proper influence from what is not, it's essential to have a thorough understanding of the construct. To *influence* is to encourage someone or something toward a particular end. That encouragement may be intentional or unintentional. Parents purposefully do and say things to encourage their children to do well in school, like helping them with their homework and telling them the importance of good grades for getting into college. In addition, by their own work habits and self-discipline, parents often unwittingly influence their children's academic success, or lack thereof. The charge for marketers, of course, is to exert intentional positive influence. Marketers must also recognize, however, the unintended influence their organizations create.

It should be noted from the above description that influence does not compel or obligate someone to take a particular action. Influence is persuasive, but not coercive; it respects and retains individual volition. While influence encourages people to act in a particular way, it also allows them the discretion to decide how or whether to respond. Above all, what should be taken away from the preceding discussion is that influence is inherently a good thing. Of course, there's such a thing as bad influence. Most of us, however, have been much more greatly impacted by positive influences. Influence is one of the main ways we learn. God brings us into this world pretty much as *tabula rasa*, a clean slate. Through the influence of a variety of individuals and institutions, however, we learn all sorts of essential information and skills that allow us to function effectively in society. Some of that influence comes from individuals like family members and friends. Other influence comes from organizations like schools, churches, and companies.

Personally, I'm grateful for positive influence from all sources, whether commercial or noncommercial. I'm thankful that my wife influences me to slow down and enjoy life. I'm thankful that my kids influence me to play and have fun. I also appreciate businesses that influence me to purchase products that make my work more productive, my food taste better, and my aging body feel less pain. Marketing influence is a good thing for consumers, provided that it preserves informed consent—one of the two key prerequisites for mutually beneficial exchange.

Marketing influence should be desirable to consumers for two main reasons. First, consumers *need* marketing influence because most consumers, particularly retail consumers, operate at an informational disadvantage. As important as consumption decisions may be for people, it's not their day job. Many other thoughts and activities rightly occupy their time and attention. Organizations' very existence, in contrast, tends to be intimately tied to the products and services they market. Consequently, firms expend considerable time and resources to become experts on the goods with which they deal. Over time the aggregate result of this focus is a tremendous informational advantage for organizations over most of the consumers they serve.

Given this imbalance, consumers need marketers to explain features, answer questions about benefits, and generally steer them on the right path. As a consumer, I've realized my informational inadequacy on many occasions and have greatly appreciated the assistance I've received from conscientious marketers. Buying new technology and getting our cars repaired are a couple of examples that come quickly to mind. Of course, with this surplus of information and expertise comes the responsibility for marketers to treat consumers well.

Second, consumers not only need marketing influence, they also often *want* it. Even in cases where they could make their own informed choice, consumers sometimes seek out marketing influence. For example, when my wife and I eat at a restaurant we've never been to before (which doesn't happen often enough!), we frequently ask the waiter or waitress what they recommend. You might think their response would be, "Oh, everything is good," but surprisingly they normally make very specific and helpful recommendations, and we usually follow them. In any case, the point is that we ask for this influence into our dinner choice.

> Consumers want to be influenced in ways that will benefit them.

Certain trends in social media also support the notion that consumers often want marketing influence. On Facebook thousands of people "Like" companies and their products. Of course, some of the motivation behind these commercial connections is that individuals want to reveal their preferences and express their personalities to their friends. Often, however, individuals specifically want to receive communication from their favorite organizations. They want to learn about the companies' new products and to be made aware of sales or other specials. They also want to receive good customer service. In short, consumers want to be influenced in ways that will benefit them.

To summarize this chapter's main points, marketing is the science that seeks to facilitate mutually beneficial exchange, which is based on both parties receiving fair value that they have purposefully chosen. The value in an exchange is primarily a function of *product, price,* and *place. Promotion,* or marketing communication, provides some secondary value to the exchange; however, its main contribution comes in the form of influence, i.e., its ability to initiate the exchange and to impact it positively along the way and afterward. As the preceding discussion has suggested, marketing is about more than influencing consumers; for instance it also involves understanding what target market members need, and it includes delivering products where and when they want to consume them. Still, influence encompasses a very large portion of marketers' work and is likely the most pervasive component, which is the reason it is the focus of this book.

As I mentioned in the first chapter, much of this book will examine objectionable forms of influence. It's important to note, therefore, two things: 1) that there are other ethical issues in marketing outside of those involving influence, and 2) that any unscrupulous practices done in the name of marketing are aberrations of the discipline. As I've argued above, true marketing benefits both buyers and sellers, and legitimate marketing influence is a good thing: the vast majority of ways in which marketers influence are appropriate and desirable. The need, therefore, is not to try to work within a narrow range of acceptable influence, but rather to recognize and avoid a small set of behavioral influence that scripture identifies as unacceptable.

So, we'll first turn our attention to the seven categories of inappropriate influence that every person, including every marketer, should eschew. After an opening vignette and other examples, each of these seven chapters (two through nine) offers a biblical perspective of the focal behavior and ends with additional examples of how a marketer can enact influence that's God-honoring. Since this book's primary audience involves Christians who care about marketing, Chapter Ten explores the related topic of "Marketing and the Church." Likewise, because many Christians, marketers and others, find themselves working in organizations and industries that are not Christian-owned and operated, Chapter Eleven offers advice for "Christians in a Secular Workplace." Lastly, Chapter Twelve provides some summative thoughts and a final conclusion to this book's unique topic.

Reflection Questions – Marketing & Influence

1. To what extent do you believe marketing is "mutually beneficial"?

2. What do you think are some of the most common misconceptions about marketing?

3. Is influence a positive, negative, or neutral concept?

4. What are some of the main ways in which marketing influences others?

5. Do you ever seek influence? When, or why?

PART 2:

THE SEVEN SINS OF INFLUENCE

There are some words that always have positive connotations, like *love*—it's hard to imagine "bad love." Likewise, there are words that always have negative associations, like *evil*—there's no such thing as "good evil." As most of us have experienced, and as Chapter Two suggested, *influence* is a concept that can be either positive or negative depending upon a variety of factors such as its purpose and execution.

Chapters Three through Nine elucidate seven types of influence gone wrong. In identifying this short list of inappropriate influence, however, the implication is that all other influence is good. So, by avoiding the sinful varieties, one ensures that his or her influence honors God and shows love to others.

The other important implication is that these "Seven Sins" are not the exclusive realm of marketers. Any person can fall prey to the temptation to deceive, coerce, manipulate, etc. A core role of marketing, however, is to enact influence, which makes the discussion that follows particularly important for the discipline.

Chapter 3
FIRST SIN: DECEPTION

Truth lives on in the midst of deception.

—Friedrich von Schiller

"**C**ongratulations, you've won!" the letter said. Inside the envelope was an 8" x 10" glossy color photo of a new car and a car key. Mallory couldn't have been more excited. She'd recently passed her driver's test, and now she'd have her very own vehicle like many of her friends whose parents could afford to buy them new cars. No need to borrow Mom and Dad's relic. All she had to do was go to the auto dealership between 9:00 am and noon this coming Saturday and claim her prize. Mallory awoke early Saturday morning and rushed to the dealership.

> *Mallory:* [Beaming with excitement and holding her key like an Olympic gold medal.] "I'm here to get my car."
>
> *Sales Manager:* "Okay, right this way, young lady."
>
> *The Sales Manager leads Malory to a shiny red coupe, parked in the middle of the showroom, like a museum exhibit.*
>
> *Sales Manager:* "Go ahead, open the door."
>
> *Almost shaking, Mallory grasps the driver's door handle and gives it a gentle pull. The door doesn't move. She steadies herself and tries again.*
>
> *Mallory:* "I think it's locked."
>
> *Sales Manager:* "Yes, you need to use your key."

Mallory blushes then quickly takes the key and inserts it into the door. She tries repeatedly to get it to turn but it won't.

Mallory: "It's not working."

Sales Manager: "That's too bad; I guess you don't get the car."

Mallory: Stunned and in disbelief. "What do you mean? The letter said I won a car."

Sales Manager: "The letter did say you won, but it didn't say you won a *car.*"

Mallory: "But there was a big picture of a car and a car key. And, it told me to bring the key here to claim my prize."

Sales Manager: "Don't worry, you did win *something.* Let me see your key."

Completely deflated, Mallory hands the Sales Manager her key. He turns it over and, trying to sound as upbeat as possible, reads a three digit code.

Sales Manager: "Three-Nine-Five. Alright, you've actually won *two* things: a free car wash and a free test drive of this new model."

Mallory: "But I don't have a car, and I don't feel like test driving this one now."

Mallory turns away and walks out of the dealership in tears.

Deception Described

Unfortunately, this story is based on the actual experience of a young woman I know. I'm glad to say she's since recovered from the ordeal; however, she's unlikely to forget how one organization abused its marketing influence. Instances like these are also regrettable because they propagate an inaccurate perception of the entire discipline and tarnish the reputation of marketers who have integrity.

Of course, it's not hard to recognize that Mallory was wronged, but what was the specific means by which she was she taken advantage? Mallory was *deceived.* Hill describes deception as encouraging someone to believe something that you don't believe yourself (2008, p. 129).

For reasons that I will explain below, I will add to this definition the notion that the deception works to the detriment of the communication's recipient. Taken together, this understanding of deception fits Mallory's situation very well. The car dealership encouraged Mallory and many other recipients of the direct mail piece to believe that they were new car winners. All the while, the dealership's management knew the incredible odds of anyone winning a car. The managers encouraged Mallory to believe something they didn't believe themselves, to her detriment. For the dealership, the deceptive promotion promised to increase foot traffic in the showroom, possibly leading to a few more test drives and perhaps a couple of vehicle purchases. For Mallory, the results of the deception were time wasted, shattered hopes, and emotional trauma.

Deception in the Bible

Even for those who are relatively unfamiliar with the Bible, it's likely no surprise to hear that Christian scripture condemns deception. In fact, biblical admonishments of deception are rather numerous and unambiguous, for instance:

- "Do not steal. Do not lie. Do not deceive one another" (Leviticus 19:11).

- "For, whoever would love life and see good days must keep his tongue from evil and his lips from deceitful speech" (1 Peter 3:10).

- "The wisdom of the prudent is to give thought to their ways, but the folly of fools is deception" (Proverbs 14:8).

In addition, Paul is quick to emphasize that he never used deception in his work of spreading the Gospel and influencing others for

Christ (2 Corinthians 4:1-2). A powerful lesson against deception can also be taken from the tragic case of Ananias and Saphira. Their decision to deceive others by suggesting that they were giving all of the money earned from the sale of their property to the Church led to the couple's untimely demise (Acts 5:1-11). Of course, one also should remember the ninth commandment, found in Exodus 20:16. The instruction to "not give false testimony against your neighbor" is an indictment against lying, which represents a specific form of deception.

It is important to note here that while deception generally involves the communication of false information, the conveyance of partial information (i.e., some but not all), does not necessarily constitute deception. For instance, if a small electrical fire starts in the projection room of a movie theater, the staff might turn on the house lights and tell people to leave quickly and orderly, rather than adding "there's a fire." Although the later statement provides more complete and accurate information, it can be argued that people don't need to know why they were asked to leave until they get outside. Plus, revealing the reason for the evacuation before it's complete could cause unnecessary anxiety and even incite a panic.

You might be thinking, "Okay, I understand that example, but how could withholding marketing information be beneficial to consumers in more normal situations?" One of the most common points of applicability involves product information. Yes, as consumers we want to know the salient facts about an item so we can make a good purchase decision, but do we really want to know every bit of information that a manufacturer or retailer could potentially tell us, for instance, how long it took to make the product, the name of the person who assembled it, or the shipping company that delivered it to the store? Personally, I'm glad to not have to expend unnecessary time and energy processing more than the pertinent facts.

One also can find biblical support for the practice of limited disclosure from the life of Jesus. In several instances in which Christ healed people, he told them not to tell anyone what he had done (Matthew

8:4; Mark 7:36; Luke 5:14; Luke 8:56). At times Jesus also instructed his disciples not to tell others who he was or what they witnessed
(Matthew 16:20; Matthew 17:9; Mark 8:30; Luke 9:21). Why did Jesus
on occasion restrict communication? We can't
know the specifics, but we can be sure it was to
help others and to serve the Father's greater purpose. Few, if any, would argue that Jesus acted
immorally in these cases, so the withholding
of information can't be categorically deceptive.

*The withholding of
information can be moral if
it serves others' interests.*

Getting back to my qualifier of Hill's (2008) definition of deception,
I believe what distinguishes these Messianic cases, as well as the other
two examples described above, is that the communication is not to the
recipients' detriment; rather, the partial disclosure is for their ultimate
benefit. The withholding of information can be moral if it serves the
interests of others.

Deception in Marketing

It's time to take the conversation back to deception and marketing. What are examples of marketing practices that are deceptive?
Unfortunately, thanks to those who engage in unscrupulous marketing, an abundance of illustrations exist. The case of Mallory and the
new car is just one. Like the auto dealership, certain companies take
the short-sighted approach of trying to trick consumers into choosing
them, with the hope that the deception will either go unnoticed or be
tolerated.

Another common form of deception involves marketing communication that highlights extraordinary customer results, making it
seem like most users can expect the same exceptional outcomes that
a small set of unique users have enjoyed. Weight loss ads, showcas-
ing people who have lost 50 or 75 lbs. have been notorious in this
regard. Fortunately, the Federal Trade Commission (FTC) has tight-
ened restrictions surrounding the use of ad disclaimers like "results not

typical," which has served as a legal barrier to such misrepresentations (FTC Guides, 2009). Still, there is always the potential for unprincipled organizations to mislead consumers by suggesting unrealistic or improbable benefits, such as an ad that shows a young man suddenly becoming irresistible to the opposite sex after he starts using a certain body wash.

For salespeople, there can be a wide variety of temptations to deceive. In order to win a new account, a salesperson may feel compelled to lead a prospect to believe that his company has extensive experience in a certain type of business, which it does not. It also can be tempting for a salesperson to withhold information about additional costs like shipping, installation, or maintenance. In these cases, partial disclosure works to the detriment of the customer and *does* constitute deception. Salespeople also should be wary of deceiving customers by creating a false sense of urgency, for instance, by saying that someone else wants to buy the same product or that there will soon be a price increase. If these statements are not true, the salesperson is lying, which is always deceptive. If true, there's still the potential that such statements constitute coercion, which is discussed in Chapter Four.

> *The problem with stealth influence is that it encourages consumers to let down their perceptual guard.*

A subcategory of deceptive influence might be called *stealth*. It involves marketing promotion that's disguised to appear as something else, thereby avoiding detection by consumer "radar." Advertorials are one example of stealth promotion: As you read the newspaper you come across an interesting story about the Amish making space heaters. Upon closer inspection, however, you see the small, obligatory word *advertisement*. Product placement is another tactic that might be considered stealth: As you watch your favorite television program, you notice that one of the show's main characters uses an Apple MacBook. Stealth influence is not restricted to mass media. One such example involves disguising promotion as research: You get a phone call from a person who works for a "political action organization;" he asks if you'd complete a brief survey about your political views. The first question is: "Do you think Mark Stevens' ten years of experience as a successful businessman, his extensive volunteer work, and his strong family values make him a good candidate for state legislature?" The remaining questions are similar veiled attempts to create a favorable impression of the candidate and to generate votes for him.

The problem with stealth influence is that it encourages consumers to let down their perceptual guard as they think they're receiving product information from a non-commercial, unbiased source. Most of us will interpret a recommendation related to a particular technology brand much differently if it comes from a good friend versus from an agent of the tech company. There's not necessarily anything wrong with a promotional message from the tech firm, it's just that we'd like to know that the company is the source so we can judge the message accordingly. In determining whether a particular marketing tactic represents stealth influence, therefore, the pivotal question seems to be "Why does the organization believe it's necessary for its communication to *not* be perceived as promotion?" If the firm is attempting to gain an unfair advantage that will work to the detriment of consumers, then stealth influence and deception are occurring.

The good news is that successfully following the marketing concept does not require deception.

Non-Deceptive Influence

The good news is that successfully following the marketing concept does not require deception. In fact, deception is antithetical to facilitating mutually beneficial exchange and long-term relationships. People will generally avoid doing business with parties who they know act deceptively. Fortunately, the vast majority of marketing influence is effectively exercised without deception. For a marketer who has developed a total product concept that meets the target market's needs, truth is the most powerful promotion.

Along the lines of legitimate marketing influence, there are a few marketing practices that may at first glance raise a red flag, but generally do not entail deception. I'm reminded of a television commercial in which a swimmer uses a certain brand of razor to shave all the hair off his head and body before a race. When the starter's gun sounds, he jumps off the blocks and into the water. His body is so smooth and frictionless that within a couple of seconds he squirts like a dolphin through the water and right out the other end of the pool, hitting his head on the opposite wall. Some may look at this ad and say it's deceptive because no one can swim that fast. Reasonable consumers, however, quickly recognize the over-the-top exaggeration as humor, not realism. The fact that no one could possibly swim that fast makes the ad funny. At the same time, the ad conveys a legitimate benefit of using the razor—a close shave. The FTC considers this type of exaggeration legal, calling it *puffery* (FTC Policy, 1983). Clear puffery is not deceptive

For a marketer who has developed a total product concept that meets the target market's needs, truth is the most powerful promotion.

As mentioned above, partial disclosure of product information also should not be considered categorically deceptive. If the details withheld are of no use to consumers in their decision making, then organizations do consumers a service by limiting the amount of information they need to process. I'm personally very thankful for individuals and organizations that can concisely tell me the important facts I need to know, while screening the details I would find superfluous.

Finally, some people believe it's deceptive for a company to promote the same features or benefits as does one or more of its competitors. The implication here seems to be that a firm shouldn't highlight a positive attribute unless it's the only company that can make the claim. My response to this belief is "Why not?" If a job candidate claims that she's a hard worker, I don't interpret her as saying she is the only hard-working prospective employee, nor that she is the most hard-working one. As long as an organization doesn't illegitimately claim exclusivity or superiority, it's not deceptive for it to promote positive features it has in common with other firms.

When I ask my students for examples of unethical marketing, many of the responses fall under the umbrella of deception. I have clarified what deception is, why it's wrong, and how marketers can avoid it. Likewise, this discussion has sought to affirm that there is a broad array of effective marketing communication that is not deceptive. In fact, marketing not only has no need to deceive, deception is antithetical to the discipline.

> **Influence Tip #1**: To avoid deception, don't lead people to believe something that you don't believe yourself and that would cause them harm if they acted on that untruth.

Reflection Questions – Deception

1. How would you describe deception?

2. What is the relationship between deception and lying?

3. Is deception always immoral, or are there instances in which it is okay or even desirable to deceive?

4. What examples of deceptive marketing have you seen?

5. Do consumers ever deceive marketers, and if so, how?

Chapter 4
SECOND SIN: COERCION

People are changed, not by coercion or intimidation, but by example.

–Source Unknown

We first noticed the water in the carpeting near the couch. Initially there was just a little wetness. We weren't even sure what it was from. Maybe someone had spilled something. We put down some old towels to absorb the water. As the wetness increased, however, we soon realized that the basement of our house, which we had purchased only a year or so earlier, was flooding.

As the abnormally heavy April rains continued, the water problem grew worse. A large portion of the basement carpeting was now saturated. We knew we had to do something to take care of the problem, especially since our basement was our family room—the place where we watched TV and played with our two young children. We decided to call some basement waterproofing companies.

Not an hour after we called, a representative from the first company arrived. I thought it was interesting, and in retrospect a little peculiar, that just as we were welcoming him inside a call came on his cellphone from his wife. He talked with her for a minute or two while we stood waiting and listening to his side of the conversation. When he finished, we briefly described the problem, he asked if we had spoken with any other companies, and we led him downstairs to see the damage firsthand.

After doing a brief inspection, he turned to us with a look of dread.

Water-proofer: "This is not good."
Us: "What is it?"
Water-proofer: "Deadly mold will grow in these conditions."
Us: [speechless]
Water-proofer: "Do you have children playing down here?"
Us: "Yes." [Although, I wasn't sure why he had to ask this question, with toys lying all around and our daughter peering nearby.]
Water-proofer: "You better get this taken care of right away." [Implication—if you want your kids to live]
Us: "Okay."
Water-proofer: "Unfortunately, we're booked solid for at least the next month."
Us: "Oh, no."
Water-proofer: "Unless . . ."
Us: "Unless what?"
Water-proofer: "Unless there happens to be a cancellation. Let me call Cindy at our office and see if anything has come open."
He calls, chats for a couple of minutes, and turns to talk with us.
Water-proofer: "You're in luck. We have one opening this Friday. It's likely to be gone soon, though, so you need to reserve it right now."

He pulled out a contract. We were reluctant to sign anything so quickly, and for such a large amount of money, but we decided to do so, given the sense of urgency and feeling of imminent danger. We also found that we could cancel the contract during the next 48 hours if necessary.

Later that day we met with representatives from two other water-proofing companies. Neither of these men described our situation as being nearly so hazardous. Also, their estimates were about half as much as that of the first company. We soon realized that we'd been taken advantage of by our first visitor. So, we canceled that contract and had the work done by one of the other companies. Thankfully, our basement stayed dry from then on. We still haven't forgotten about this experience, and will long remember how it felt to be coerced.

Coercion Described

What is coercion? As the preceding example illustrates, coercion involves pressuring people to do something against their will. Maybe you're thinking, "But you wanted to fix the problem and get your basement waterproofed." Yes, we did; however, we also wanted a reasonable amount of time to make an informed choice of contractor, and we didn't want to make the decision under intense emotional pressure. Both of these tactics led us to feel coerced.

Coercion differs markedly from deception. In fact, the two are almost opposites. With deception, individuals are free to make any decision they'd like; however, they're not given adequate, truthful information. In contrast, when people are coerced they often have complete information, but they're made to feel that they have no choice but the alternative presented to them—the proverbial gun-to-the head situation. Coercion takes away or weakens an individual's volition, or free will.

As the waterproofing example suggested, one of the most effective forms of coercion involves emotional pressure. The consumer decision-making process is generally a rational one. People recognize a problem or need, seek relevant information, identify alternatives that meet the need, compare alternatives on the relevant attributes, and make a choice (Hawkins & Mothersbaugh, 2010). Of course, God *has* created us as emotional beings, too. We have the ability to feel love, joy, fear, anger, etc. We are not exclusively rational creatures (like Star Trek's Mr. Spock), so it's natural and appropriate for emotions to enter into

> Coercion differs markedly from deception. In fact, the two are almost opposites.

our decision-making. There's nothing wrong, for instance, for a young girl to want an aqua-colored backpack because she likes aqua. Likewise, there's nothing wrong with a marketer making good quality backpacks in several colors and advertising: "choose your favorite shade."

What *is* wrong is for a marketer or anyone else to use emotions to dictate decisions for individuals. To do so creates a lack of control, or choice, that's similar to going to your doctor's office, sitting on the examination table, and having her tap your knee with the reflex hammer. You don't intend for your lower leg to jerk upward, but it does. The response is out of your control. In the same way, heavy-handed emotional appeals can spur knee-jerk reactions by consumers, circumventing rational decision-making and causing people to make choices they otherwise would not.

> *Emotional appeals can spur knee-jerk reactions by consumers, circumventing rational decision-making and causing people to make choices they otherwise would not make.*

Coercion in the Bible

Like deception, coercion certainly doesn't seem like something God would endorse; nevertheless, it's more challenging to identify scripture that deals with coercion than with deception, mainly because coercion is not a common biblical word. Further study reveals, however, that coercion is not consistent with scripture. Since the beginning with Adam and Eve, God has given humankind free will and allowed individuals to choose whether or not to follow Him. If God preserves the freedom to choose, it seems that we should do the same.

This absence of coercion can be seen through examples such as Paul using reason, not force or emotion, to persuade Jews and Greeks to believe the Gospel (Acts 18:4). Likewise, Jesus talking with the Samaritan woman (John 4:1-26), healing the sick (Matthew 14:14; Mark 1:34; Luke 4:40), and speaking with Nicodemus (John 3:1-21), support the idea that Jesus used dialogue and empathy, not coercion, in sharing the good news.

Where examples of coercion can be found in the Bible, they are committed by individuals who appear *not* to be following God. Using prolonged emotional battery, Delilah coerced Samson to reveal the secret of his strength (Judges 16:4-22). Under threat of death in a fiery furnace, Nebuchadnezzar forced many people to worship his idol; although Shadrach, Meshach, and Abednego did not concede (Daniel 3:1-30). Also, one of the most infamous examples of coercion in scripture involved the Jewish leaders pressuring Pilate to crucify Jesus by publicly questioning the Roman governor's loyalty to Caesar (John 19:12-16).

Coercion in Marketing

As the preceding examples illustrate, coercion often leverages negative emotions such as fear (loss of reward, threat of punishment, or worse) and guilt ("How could you live with yourself?" or "If you really loved me..."). These same types of appeals are sometimes the tools of misguided marketers abusing their influence. We've already seen this intimidation in the story of the waterproofing company; we'll now consider a few others.

Our nation is blessed to have an array of socially-minded organizations capable in many different ways of helping people who lack skills, resources, or a viable support network. Since the beneficiaries are normally not in a position to pay for the nonprofits' services, the organizations rely on the contributions of donors to support their work. Most of the appeals to potential benefactors are entirely appropriate: The nonprofits present a realistic picture of the need, identify the resources that will help, and describe the positive outcomes that will likely result, including probable benefits for the supporters, such as the satisfaction of helping others or peace from living in a better community or world.

Occasionally, however, nonprofit appeals take a much more emotionally aggressive tact and coercive tenor. Imagine the end of a television commercial in which the camera pans across a group of destitute people, many of whom are sitting on the sunbaked ground. The picture zooms in and remains on the face of one specific child with an extremely distressed look. Over a background of soft, somber music, the narrator says:

> "You might be grateful that this little boy isn't your child, but he *is* your child. The fact that you're watching this program means you have the ability and resources to help the world's children."

> "You've been given so much. He has so little. Life has treated him unfairly. You are his sole hope for justice. Don't deny your responsibility. Help now."

Unfortunately many of the organizations that employ overbearing tactics like the preceding ones represent legitimate causes and people who really do need help. It's regrettable because coercing action through fear and guilt can do more harm than good. Over time, these negative tactics are likely to taint the reputations of the nonprofits that use them, making the organizations less attractive to donors. Also, when people are motivated by fear or guilt, they often give just enough to allay those feelings; whereas, when motivation is positive, the sky is the limit in terms of how generously an individual might respond. Finally, coercive appeals using fear or guilt may cause certain people who should *not* respond, to take action, such as an elderly widow living on a meager income.

The preceding arguments against coercive appeals rest largely on the negative outcomes that often result from such tactics. As the biblical examples discussed earlier suggested, however, even positive ends do not justify coercive means. Despite the fact that people can be led to act out of fear and guilt, it's still wrong to do so, primarily because such coercive tactics prohibit individuals from making unencumbered, rational choices. These tactics deny a person his or her free will.

In a business-to-business context, *reciprocity* can pose a temptation for firms to resort to coercion. Reciprocity is the practice of two firms buying each other's products, thereby becoming customers of one another. Reciprocity can be a good prac-tice if both companies genuinely benefit from their purchases; that is, they find their counterpart's products to be true, competitively-based values. Like indi-viduals, organizations should be free to make purchase decisions on their own merits. It would be coercive, therefore, for reciprocity to be made a condition of sale. Company A shouldn't agree to pur-chase products from Company B only if Company B will buy products from Company A. Such a stipulation represents the threat of a reward withheld, or an appeal to fear ("we'll lose the order"), which is coercive.

> *Marketing influence should never act as a heavy hand, pushing people against their will toward a choice. Instead, marketing influence should consist of holding consumers' hands and helping them get to where they want to go.*

Another fear appeal that is sometimes used against business-to-business customers and end consumers is the threat of a significant price increase. First, however, a qualification should be made: If ac-count executives or sales associates know for a fact that a substantial price increase is imminent, it's a courtesy for them to inform custom-ers. As a consumer, I would appreciate knowing; yet I wouldn't nec-essarily expect to be told. The example I'd like to put forward here, though, represents largely the opposite dynamic. In this case, the com-pany agent has no express knowledge of an impending price increase; nevertheless, he tells the customer that she "better buy now because you never know when prices might go up." There's not necessarily anything untrue or deceptive about this statement; prices often do in-crease. Statements like these are likely, however, to create unnecessary anxiety in consumers and make them feel pressured to purchase before they're ready. A similar appeal to fear, or threat of a missed opportunity, occurs when unscrupulous marketers unnecessarily mention to consumers that someone else might buy the product if they don't ("At such a great price, this one won't last long").

Non-Coercive Influence

As the preceding examples suggest, there's often a fine line between coercive and legitimate marketing influence. I admit, many situations are gray for me. In keeping with the discussion near the beginning of this chapter, appeals to emotion are not always wrong. Given that we are emotional beings, it would be strange for all advertising or other marketing communication to be devoid of emotion, particularly emotions that are relevant to the product's unique benefit proposition.

Let's consider further appeals to fear. Sometimes fear is actually a positive benefit. It's hard for me to understand personally, but some people like to be scared. For them a terrifying rollercoaster or a frightening movie would be desirable. In most instances, however, fear is a negative motivator; that is, people buy certain products so they don't have to be afraid. There's not necessarily anything wrong with this use of fear, provided that it's not overplayed, thereby crossing the line into coercion. Many of us have seen the television ads of home security companies. It's natural for people to fear a break-in of their homes. It's also likely that owning a home security system will allay some of that fear. Consequently, it's appropriate for home security companies to promote the mitigation of fear as a product benefit. The issue, then, becomes exactly how that benefit is communicated. It would be fine, for instance, for an ad to feature a testimonial in which a customer described how she used to be afraid at night, but now she enjoys much greater peace with her home security system.

At the other extreme, it would be coercive for a television ad to show an intruder attacking a woman in her home, with narration urging, "Don't let this happen to you." On one hand, the ad would not be untrue. Attacks like the one illustrated *do* occur, but they are so rare and unlikely to happen to any given individual that there's no reason for people to live in fear of them. Furthermore, graphic images like these can easily spawn unfounded fears that cause people to act irrationally: I'm reminded of a person I know who after seeing the movie *Jaws* as a young girl was afraid to get out of her bed and step on the floor.

No one likes to be coerced; if you like the influence, it's probably not coercion. It makes no sense, therefore, for marketers, who are charged with meeting consumers' needs and giving them what they like, to employ coercion. Marketing is about creating a mutually beneficial exchange; consequently, marketing influence should never act as a heavy hand, pushing people against their will toward a choice. Instead, marketing influence should consist of holding consumers' hands and helping them get to where *they* want to go.

Influence Tip #2: To avoid coercion, don't do anything that takes away an individual's ability to make a free, rational choice.

Reflection Questions – Coercion

1. How are coercion and deception different?

2. Why are emotional appeals usually more coercive than rational appeals?

3. Is coercive influence ever acceptable?

4. When have you felt coerced, inside or outside a marketing context?

5. How can marketers be persuasive without being coercive?

Chapter 5
THIRD SIN: MANIPULATION

Love comes when manipulation stops.

—Joyce Brothers

Have you ever experienced a situation in which the behavior of someone close to you took you completely by surprise, and not in a good way? You may have felt like saying afterward, "Wow, I thought you were my friend," or "mother," or "pastor," or "therapist," whatever the case may have been! I had such a situation recently in which an organization to which I'm close perpetrated such surprising and *not* so good behavior. Here's what happened…

I received an email from the organization, announcing an upcoming online seminar. The topic of the event interested me, so I thought I might participate, but I wanted to know how much the seminar would cost. I reread the email to see if I had missed that significant piece of information. When I still didn't see a cost, I decided to click on a button to "Learn More."

The link took me to the event homepage. I scoured the page but still found no listing of cost or any obvious links to it. So, I decided to click on the link to register for the event, thinking that the cost would surely be listed there—I was wrong. Instead, the organization asked me to enter an array of personal information including my name, address, phone number, and email address. At that point I felt I was being manipulated and decided I was no longer interested in attending the event.

What makes this type of approach manipulative is that many people undoubtedly continue beyond my point of despair. When the cost of the event finally does appear, a screen or two later, prospective registrants are probably unlikely to back out, even if the cost is more than they expected. Their reasoning may be that they've already invested time and effort into registering, and they've already submitted their personal information.

Now here's what I'm really embarrassed to say: The organization that used this tactic is one of our nation's largest associations of marketers. Hopefully this approach to the event registration was an oversight, or a slip-up. Negligence would be a little more palatable than malicious intent.

Like deception and coercion, *manipulation* is a word that rarely has a positive connotation, unless you're involved in mathematics and manipulating things like roots and exponents. Otherwise, manipulation may be thought of as *scheming to achieve an outcome that would not otherwise be chosen.* If you're thinking that manipulation seems a little bit like deception and a little bit like coercion, you're right. There's a resemblance to both prior sins. The way I think about it, if deception and coercion had a child, their offspring would be manipulation. The kid has some of the DNA of both parents, yet manipulation is its own unique person.

> If deception and coercion got together and had a child, their offspring would be manipulation.

As in the registration example I just shared, manipulation doesn't necessarily involve any overt lies, yet the entire process rests on an undercurrent of deceit. Likewise, when people are manipulated, they don't necessarily take a single action that's against their will, yet the combined effect of all of the acts is an outcome they would not otherwise have chosen. In this way, manipulation is a cunningly-designed combination of understated deception and inconspicuous coercion.

Manipulation requires some fairly sophisticated planning. Deception, on the other hand, may be complex, but it can also be surprisingly simple and easy to execute. In fact, if any one of us isn't careful, we can unwittingly commit deception by something we inadvertently do or say. Likewise, coercion can be as easy as letting loose some raw emotion. It's much less probable that anyone of us will accidentally manipulate someone. Manipulation requires forethought and often the ability to implement several interdependent steps. It takes true talent to manipulate!

Manipulation in the Bible

It goes without saying that manipulation is a behavior that does not receive biblical affirmation. What does scripture say specifically about the practice? Like coercion, manipulation is not a common biblical word, which makes its study initially challenging. However, there is another phrase readily found in scripture that represents the same notion of scheming to bring about undesirable outcomes. The phrase is *plot evil*. Here are several examples of its repudiation:

- "Do not those who plot evil go astray? But those who plan what is good find love and faithfulness" (Proverbs 14:22).

- "Woe to those who plan iniquity, to those who plot evil on their beds! At morning's light they carry it out because it is in their power to do it" (Micah 2:1).

- "'Do not plot evil against your neighbor, and do not love to swear falsely. I hate all this,' declares the Lord" (Zechariah 8:17).

As one digs deeper into scripture, specific instances of manipulative behavior start to surface. Haman's plot to destroy the Jews was both deceptive and coercive, as he shrewdly manipulated King Xerxes into issuing a decree that would have delivered a death sentence to Queen Esther, as well as Mordecai, the man who had earlier saved the King's life (Esther 3:1-15). Similarly, a contingent of underlings manipulated King Darius into passing an edict against praying that was intended to lead to Daniel's death by lions (Daniel 6:1-28).

Given that Satan is known as "the father of lies" (John 8:44), it's not surprising that he is also quite adept at manipulating. One of his best known attempts at manipulation was aimed at none other than Jesus (Matthew 4:1-11). Satan's unsuccessful temptation of Jesus in the desert consisted of at least one invitation to perform an action that was not inherently wrong: eating bread. Satan also wanted Jesus to turn stones into bread, but even that act may have been acceptable for Jesus under the circumstances—he hadn't eaten for forty days and forty nights, and another time he was willing to turn water into wine (John 2:1-11). This seemingly benign invitation was Satan's first manipulative step in attempting to draw Jesus away from the Father. In asking Jesus to turn stones into bread, Satan was posturing just to get his foot in the door. If Jesus complied, he'd realize some physical satisfaction, which might make Satan a little more endearing and give his second and third temptations a better chance of success. Of course, Jesus didn't succumb to the first, second, or third temptations, and Satan's manipulation failed.

Manipulation in Marketing

The Bible opposes manipulation. What unscrupulous marketing practices might constitute manipulation? As illustrated at the beginning of this chapter, withholding a product's price until consumers have taken certain steps toward purchase is one common example. Some restaurants are notorious for this practice, not including the prices of beverages, desserts, or even entrées on their menus. A similar manipulative tactic involves delaying the disclosure of related costs like shipping, set-up, or maintenance. I'm not referring here to cases in which consumers are led to believe that all costs are included, only to be surprised to see a shipping and handling charge on their invoice. Such cases represent straightforward deception. Manipulation, in contrast, functions more subtly.

Imagine a consumer who is traveling abroad and looking in a souvenir shop at possible gifts for a family member. She tells the store's owner that she's reluctant to buy anything because she has almost no space in her luggage. He informs her that the store can ship her purchase to the U.S. They then proceed to look at several expensive clocks, which are all the same size and shape. After the customer decides on one particular clock and they're standing at the cash register, the store owner tells her that the shipping cost will be twice the cost of the clock—a detail he knew much earlier but withheld until he was confident the customer would not back out of the purchase. The customer pauses and debates whether to buy the clock; however, with the time already invested and the store owner looking on, she feels compelled to follow-through with the purchase.

The same type of manipulation can also occur for a much larger purchase and a longer time commitment. For example, an automaker offers new car buyers the option to upgrade the standard vehicle warranty to an extended bumper-to-bumper warranty. To avoid the risk of the warranty being voided, however, the car's owner must have all maintenance performed at the dealership, including expensive oil changes and an array of preventative measures that go far beyond what even most conscientious owners would deem necessary.

Closely related to the preceding example is the way in which some companies handle consumables—the key supplies that are essential for use of their main product, for instance, blades for razors (the classic example), ink cartridges for printers, and oil mix for lawn mowers. First, I should clarify that there's nothing wrong with a company making supplies to be used with its products. We'd be upset if they didn't do so and no other company did either. Likewise, firms should be entitled to make money on the sale of such supplies—we can't expect companies to give them away, or even to sell them at cost. The potential for manipulation, however, occurs based on three factors: the absolute cost of the consumables, the consumables' cost relative to the main product, and the availability of the consumables from other sources.

Owners of mechanical pencils probably do not feel manipulated in their purchase of pencil lead refills because the lead is inexpensive overall and cheap relative to the cost of the pencil. Also, lead that will work in the pencil is readily available from a number of different suppliers. On the other hand, owners of an inkjet printer are likely to feel manipulated if the printer cost $95, a tri-color ink cartridge costs $75, and no other company's ink cartridges will work in the printer. Although printer owners have not necessarily been deceived or coerced, they probably resent the considerable money they have to spend on each new ink cartridge.

Another classic manipulative tactic that some untrustworthy marketers employ is bait-and-switch. An electronics retailer advertises a certain television at a very low price. When consumers come to the store looking for the advertised set, the sales staff shows it to them, but then quickly shifts attention to a more expensive and profitable model, which the staff touts as a "far superior television." This technique begs the question: "If the other television is so much better, why didn't the store advertise *that* one?" Of course, the more expensive television's price point would not make for as enticing an advertisement. So the bait-and-switch tactic first maximizes store foot traffic. People come on their own volition to see the advertised TV, which is available at the promotional price. They're shown the set, but are then encouraged to consider a different model. There's not necessarily any deception or coercion at either stage. The total process becomes manipulative, however, as consumers are led to an outcome that they likely would not have otherwise chosen and that probably also works to their detriment.

Another variety of manipulation comes from certain multi-level marketing companies. Multi-level marketing involves a business model in which agents earn money for themselves and their organization both by selling the firm's products and by recruiting new distributors for the organization. Legitimate multi-level marketing programs do exist; they offer products that provide genuine value to customers and are based on a sustainable level of distributor recruitment. However, the potential for manipulation occurs when new distributors: are asked to pay steep initiation costs, are given unrealistic recruitment targets, and are obliged to sell and recruit mainly among family members and friends. Some multi-level programs appear to be based on a business model in which the firm's main revenue stream comes from the sale of expensive sample kits to new distributors, who are often college students. With several hundred dollars invested in a kit and with modest professional networks, students feel compelled to recruit other students and to try to sell products to their small circles of family members and friends. In addition, the distributors themselves are sometimes required to buy a certain amount of product each month. Such business practices are highly manipulative.

An age-old form of manipulation is bribery. Bribery functions by pitting the interests of agents against the interests of their principals. For instance, a sales representative from ABC wants to sell a large quantity of product to XYZ. In order to improve his chances of getting an order, he offers XYZ's purchasing agent an all-expenses-paid trip to the Bahamas. The purchasing agent now

> *Bribery functions by pitting the interests of agents against the interests of their principals.*

is inclined to place an order with ABC even though the firm may not be offering the best quality product at the best price. The purchasing agent is not being deceived or coerced—she knows what's happening and can readily say no. Instead, she is the target of a carefully choreographed scheme to get her to select an outcome that she wouldn't have otherwise chosen. She is being manipulated.

A few other examples of manipulation might involve:

- "Free" products, when consumers need to make an initial purchase and jump through various hoops in order to receive the free item

- Product obsolescence, when a company stops providing parts and service for relatively new products that it has recently discontinued

- Store layouts, when fixtures and aisle ways lead shoppers to walk through the entire store and past all its products in order to get to the cash register or exit

- Network management, when a salesperson does a favor for a client just to create a sense of obligation so the salesperson can ask for a specific favor in return

Non-manipulative Influence

Despite the numerous preceding examples, marketing is not a discipline overrun by manipulation. Instead, most of the influence that marketers employ helps rather than controls consumers. The following paragraphs describe some situations that initially might appear to be manipulative, but are quite appropriate.

First, a key part of the bait-and-switch example described above was attracting consumers to the store with a product that was priced especially low. Is it manipulative to promote low price points? I say, "No," provided that the products are available at the advertised prices and there's no intention to switch consumers to other products. It's beneficial for people to buy products they need for less money, and it's helpful for marketers to advertise that availability so consumers are aware. But, you may be thinking that after people buy the low-priced products they often continue shopping and purchase other products that aren't as aggressively priced. I say there's no problem there either.

Although the other products might not represent incredible sales, they still can be good values. Plus, consumers don't have to buy them; people are free to walk into a store, buy only the advertised products, and leave—something that I've done many times.

There also have been times when I've gone to a store to buy an advertised product only to find that there were none left. Some stores simply cover themselves for this contingency by saying things like "supplies are limited." Other stores, however, go out of their way to avoid consumer dissonance by offering rain checks, or the opportunity to buy a certain quantity of the advertised product at a later date, at the sale price. Some might argue

> *A solid or compelling argument does not constitute manipulation. Manipulation involves malicious intent and often leads to detrimental outcomes.*

that rain checks encourage consumers to go back to the store and buy more. They're right; however, I've found that stores that advertise great values and take extra steps to help me avoid missing out on special sales are stores I *want* to shop at more often. I don't feel manipulated; I feel helped.

One of the examples described above, the offer of an expensive vacation to a purchasing agent, involved bribery. I believe, however, that many gifts given in business contexts are not bribes and are not manipulative. For instance, around the middle of December, a business might send fruit baskets or candy to its best clients with a note, "Thank you for your business this past year." Such gifts are not bribes for several reasons: they're expressions of appreciation, not expectations of performance; they're nominal in cost, meaning most people aren't moved to take any dramatic action because of a fruit basket; and they're given to the entire company, not one individual.

Some people claim that all advertising is manipulative. It's hard for me to accept that argument given my understanding of manipulation. Furthermore, the three main goals of marketing promotion, including advertising, are to inform, persuade, and remind (Lamb, Hair, &

McDaniel, 2010). The first and third goals are far removed from any-thing manipulative: it's challenging to manipulate someone by objec-tively conveying information (informing) or by reiterating information that's been shared before (reminding). Persuasion, admittedly, comes closer than either of the other goals, but it still does not constitute manipulation.

Although it's true that the result of persuasion is often an outcome that would not have otherwise been chosen, persuasion doesn't involve another key part of manipulation: scheming. In persuasion, people are guided in making an informed and careful analysis of the facts and in drawing a logical conclusion. As described in Chapter Four, the Apostle Paul used persuasion in sharing the Gospel. Manipulation, in contrast, tries to lay out facts and arrange the timing of analysis in a way that will lead to an irrational decision. A solid or compelling argument does not constitute manipulation. Manipulation involves malicious intent and often leads to detrimental outcomes.

Some manipulative marketing influence will probably always exist; however, my experience suggests that most marketing influence, in-cluding advertising, is not manipulative. There are thousands of ways in which marketing can and does positively influence behavior, to the benefit of everyone involved in an exchange. Nevertheless, there are, unfortunately, ample instances of unscrupulous marketing practices that need to be identified and changed. My hope is that this discus-sion of manipulation helps toward that end.

Influence Tip #3: To avoid manipulation, don't plan to deceive or coerce.

Reflection Questions – Manipulation

1. Why is manipulation "the child" of deception and coercion?

2. Why might manipulation be considered worse than either deception or coercion?

3. Are there ever instances of good manipulation?

4. Do you feel manipulated when the same company sells both a primary product and the supplies needed to use it (e.g., printer and ink cartridges)?

5. Is multi-level marketing manipulative?

Chapter 6
FOURTH SIN: DENIGRATION

> Everything we shut our eyes to, everything we run away from,
> everything we deny, denigrate or despise, serves to defeat us
> in the end.
>
> —Henry Miller

Since he was ten years old, one of Jerry's favorite pastimes has been watching football. During the fall, Sunday afternoons were especially fun times, as Jerry and his dad would settle in front of the TV and catch the action of their favorite NFL team. Now married and himself a father, Jerry has begun to cultivate the same family tradition with his own son Jason, ten, who has developed a growing interest in the game.

The only challenge to this otherwise pleasant time of paternal bonding has been some of the commercials that air during the games. Of course, many of the products advertised are not the kind of things a ten-year-old should be using (e.g., beer). Just as concerning, however, are some of the creative strategies that certain advertisers employ. When Jerry and Jason are watching a game, Jerry's strategy for commercials is to flip to other channels, perhaps catching a couple minutes of a different game or another interesting program. Unfortunately, that strategy is not fool-proof, as Jerry found out one Sunday afternoon in early January.

Much to their delight, Jerry and Jason's favorite team had made the playoffs. Now the team was embroiled in a heated battle with one of the league's premier franchises. After four quarters of high-powered offense and numerous lead changes, regulation time was coming to an end with the score tied at 35-35. The game was so exciting and intense, it hardly seemed that father and son had spent the last three hours glued to the television. As a man in his late forties knows, however, three hours of football-watching and soda-drinking sets in motion some biological needs that cannot be denied. So, with regulation time just ended, Jerry makes a suggestion:

Jerry: "Overtime won't start for a couple of minutes; let's take a quick-break."

Jason: [Still staring at the TV; no response]

Jerry: "Jason?"

Jason: "No, Dad, I don't need to."

Jerry: "Well, how about something to eat. Mom has some snacks in the kitchen."

Jason: "I'm fine."

Jerry: [Unable to muster another suggestion and unable to contain his urge any longer, he bolts to the bathroom.]

Meanwhile Jason remains in the family room, inert, eyes fixed to the television. First comes a commercial for auto insurance, followed by an ad for a fast-food chain and another for athlete's foot powder. Jason soaks them all in, then comes the mother lode.

Two very attractive, well-proportioned young women are sitting at an open-air restaurant, enjoying each other's company and a lite beer. The conversation quickly becomes impassioned, however, as the women start to argue about which of the beer's qualities is most appealing. As the quarrel intensifies, the women waste no time stripping off their clothing, down to their tiny undergarments, and commencing an all-out physical altercation. With stunned restaurant patrons looking on, the semi-clad women repeatedly slam their bodies against each other as they wrestle into and out of a water fountain and eventually land in a vat of freshly mixed cement.

Just as the lite beer commercial starts, Jerry hustles back into the room. He glances at the TV, then at Jason, whose eyes are like saucers. Propelled by a burst of adrenalin and fear, Jerry leaps to the end of the couch where he had been sitting, grabbing for the remote. It's not there. He throws off the couch pillows and cushions—still no remote. Undistracted by his father's frantic activity, Jason remains transfixed to the screen, his mouth hanging wide open. His attempted censorship thwarted, Jerry quickly changes his tactic. He lunges backward, does a half roll, and pops up next to the television. As the beer commercial actresses wrestle in the fountain water, Jerry kneels in front of the 50" LCD TV, straining to read the small black buttons that no one ever uses. At that moment Jerry's wife enters the room with a guest, "Reverend Thompson was in the neighborhood and stopped by to say hello . . ." [her voice trails off]. Jerry turns sheepishly toward them and forces a smile. Unfortunately his head is not nearly large enough to block anyone's view of the lingerie-clad models, tussling in the wet cement.

> *Partners' cheating on their spouses not only causes great individual pain, it also denigrates the institution of marriage.*

Denigration Described

Although the preceding story is fictional, the TV commercial described was quite real. In fact, when the ad aired it generated a ground-swell of response. Not surprising, some who saw the spot loved it and hoped it would be the first in a series of similar ads. Many other viewers, however, voiced their concerns, perhaps some having experienced situations similar to Jerry's.

Scores of commercials promote beer without stirring nearly as much backlash, so what was wrong with this ad? It wasn't so much the product advertised that was offensive, as the method used to promote it. Viewers apparently did not appreciate such candid and arousing sexual images, especially not during television programming that was likely to attract a demographically diverse audience. More specifically, people objected to the ad because of its multifaceted *denigration*. The ad particularly denigrated women by trivializing their personhood and reducing them to objects of sexual desire. The commercial also denigrated viewers by compelling them to witness a crude erotic spectacle. Likewise, the ad denigrated the communication process itself by shrouding the message in over-charged sexuality, which inhibited receivers' abilities to objectively interpret the commercial content.

Denigration can be described as *cheapening the inherent worth of people or things*. On the basis of their humanity, all people deserve to be treated with decency and respect. To denigrate people is to strip them of the fundamental dignity everyone deserves. Some of the most blatant examples of human denigration occurred during the Holocaust and are depicted in the Oscar-winning film *Schindler's List* (Lustig, Molen, & Spielberg, 1995). Nazis viewed Jews as second-class citizens or even as sub-human. Besides the indiscriminate killing, some of the film's most indelible images involve Jews stripped of their clothing and marched around naked with no regard for privacy or modesty.

Although the primary focus of denigration here is people, we should also recognize the potential for denigration of non-persons: both living and non-living, tangible and intangible things. For instance, breeding dogs or roosters to fight not only endangers these animals, it also relegates their existence to the satisfaction of morbid human pleasure. Littering on a pristine beach both diminishes its natural beauty and reduces the beach to a kind of garbage container. Likewise, partners' cheating on their spouses not only causes great individual pain, it also denigrates the institution of marriage.

Denigration in the Bible

The preceding examples offer some support for why it's wrong to denigrate people and things, but what does the Bible say about denigration?

As has been the case for several other Sins, the specific verb *denigrate* does not appear in scripture. This absence, however, does not denote indifference to the behavior. There are a couple of key synonyms and antonyms that paint a rather clear picture of biblical indictment of the practice.

Closely related to denigration is the act of showing *contempt*, a behavior that scripture resolutely condemns. Most of us don't use the word contempt very often in our everyday conversations; however, we may have heard of someone *casting a contemptuous glance*; or, we may have watched a television legal drama in which a judge cited an individual for *contempt of court*. Both of these examples help to correlate contempt and denigration. A person's contemptuous glance suggests disdain for the recipient and diminishes his self-worth. People are found to be in contempt of court because they have violated some aspect of the legal proceedings or disparaged courtroom decorum, thereby denigrating the judicial system.

The Bible contains numerous passages and verses that condemn the showing of contempt, thereby forbidding denigration. One of the most poignant examples involves the sons of Eli the priest, Hophni and Phinehas, who received divine judgment for sleeping with the women who served at the Tent of Meeting and for abusing the rights of pilgrims who came to offer sacrifices to God (I Samuel 2:12-34; 4:1-11). More specifically, the two young men were deemed guilty of "treating the Lord's offering with contempt" (I Samuel 2:17). Unfortunately, Hophni and Phinehas hadn't learned from the mistake of their ancestors Nadab and Abihu, sons of Aaron the priest, who also died because they denigrated God's standards for worship (Leviticus 10:1-7). In addition, the entire tribe of Ephraim was judged guilty of violating any number of commands and of generally showing contempt toward God (Hosea 12:1-14).

Of course, the Bible is not comprised solely of negative injunctions ("Don't show contempt"). Scripture is replete with positive commands, exhorting believers to do the right thing. In terms of denigration, the opposite injunction is to show honor or respect: "He who oppresses the poor shows contempt for their Maker, but whoever is kind to the needy honors God" (Proverbs 14:31). Likewise, the first commandment with a promise implores followers of God to honor their parents: "Honor your father and your mother, so that you may live long in the land the Lord your God is giving you" (Exodus 20:12). Some other scripture passages that encourage honor or respect include the following:

- "'Rise in the presence of the aged, show respect for the elderly and revere your God. I am the Lord.'" (Leviticus 19:32).

- "The Lord said to Moses, 'Tell Aaron and his sons to treat with respect the sacred offerings the Israelites consecrate to me, so they will not profane my holy name. I am the Lord'" (Leviticus 22:1-2).

- "They have harps and lyres at their banquets, tambourines and flutes and wine, but they have no regard for the deeds of the Lord, no respect for the work of his hands" (Isaiah 5:12).

- "Give everyone what you owe him: If you owe taxes, pay taxes; if revenue, then revenue; if respect, then respect; if honor, then honor" (Romans 13:7).

- "Show proper respect to everyone: Love the brotherhood of believers, fear God, honor the king" (1 Peter 2:17).

There seems to be little question that scripture condemns denigration, particularly involving our interactions with God and our relationships with other people. Moreover, the Bible also urges believers to practice positive behavior by performing actions that convey honor and respect.

Denigration in Marketing

The beer commercial described above shows how unscrupulous marketers can denigrate people and the communication process. Unfortunately, current advertising provides an array of similar examples, many of which involve lewd sexual images. Frequently this ad content demeans women in ways which are uncomfortable to describe, ranging from models in varying stages of undress to ad elements that are positioned in ways to allude to genitalia. Of course, this type of vulgarity is not limited to visual images. Some advertising copy also is very crude and sexually suggestive. A commercial for one men's hygiene product showcased two attractive female actresses using the product to clean soccer balls and golf balls in what appeared to be an infomercial setting; meanwhile they discussed the product's effectiveness in "cleaning guys' balls."

Another set of promotional tactics that denigrates the communication process involves radio and TV commercials that *yell* at consumers. Certain ads for cars and major appliances, for instance, go something like this:

> "WE'VE GOT FRIGIDAIRE, WHIRLPOOL,
> MAYTAG!!!"

> "NOBODY CAN BEAT OUR PRICES, I SAID
> NOBODY!!!"

> "DON'T WAIT ANOTHER MINUTE!!!"

> "YOU'VE GOT TO COME DOWN AND SEE
> US TODAY!!!"

"WHY ARE YOU STILL SITTING THERE? I SAID
SEE US TODAY!!!

These are the commercials that make you lunge for the TV remote or radio buttons in order to quickly cut the volume. Why do these ads resort to screaming? Well, loud noises do grab our *attention*, which is the first step in AIDA (attention, interest, desire, action) (Lamb, Hair, & McDaniel, 2010). Also, the unabashed energy sometimes succeeds in whipping consumers into an emotional frenzy, leading them to act without really thinking. Regardless of the motive, screaming at consumers in order to inform them of a purchase opportunity is always in poor taste. Besides being annoying and insulting, these ads disparage the communication process itself.

In the same way, certain other promotional tactics push the boundaries of human dignity by asking consumers to engage in particularly demeaning behavior. One of the best/worst examples occurred in China, where a retailer promised a certain car to the person who could kiss it for the longest period of time. After twenty-four hours, several participants still remained, so the contestants were instructed to stand on one leg. Finally, after twenty-seven hours kissing the car, one young woman emerged as the winner (Violet, 2007). On one hand, it's very generous to offer an expensive promotional prize like a car. On the other hand, it's demeaning to ask someone to kiss a car once, let alone do so for hours on end. Some advertisers like these kinds of promotions because of the extraordinary buzz they generate. Most of the consumers who participate in these promotions, however, are asked to sacrifice their physical comfort, time, and dignity for nothing, since only one person wins the prize. Some may argue that the contestants volunteer; that is, no one forces them to participate. That assertion is true; however, it's also likely that many of the people who engage in such promotions don't have many other options

> *It's demeaning to ask someone to kiss a car once, let alone do so for hours on end.*

for acquiring a car. Similarly, some Reality TV shows make a living off exposing the unseemly details of the lives of the participants, denigrating both the stars of the programs and the people who watch them.

As many of us can attest, promotional denigration in marketing isn't limited to mass media or public events. Denigration can also occur in an interpersonal context. For instance, I've come across salespeople who thought they could motivate potential customers through coarse language or endear them with crude humor. Such low-brow discourse degrades both the speaker and the listener, as well as the very profession of the seller, not to mention the service or product being sold.

Although marketing promotion may be the most common way in which denigration occurs, it's not the only way. Sometimes products themselves serve to degrade our humanity. For many years I worked in the specialty advertising industry, which imprints company logos and other information on products like hats, calendars, and pens. Most of the products sold in the ad specialty industry are very useful and tasteful; however, occasionally we came across a product proposition that seemed like an affront to both advertisers and product users. One supplier actually sold imprinted toilet paper. Beyond the specialty advertising industry, there are many other products that seem equally guilty of denigration. Some are degrading because of their crudeness or vulgarity. Others encourage corrupting types of behavior. Here are a few examples of denigrating products that I've observed:

- *Academic papers and degrees for purchase*: They denigrate the individuals who use them and the educational process.

- *Tobacco*: Before it kills a person through slave-like addiction, it makes users look and smell bad.

- *Undignified imprints*: We've all seen t-shirts and the like with crude pictures or sayings. One of the worst examples might be a children's lunch box that had a cartoon picture of a little girl kicking a man in his private parts.

- *Violent video games*: Glorifying violence is always a debasing activity.

- *Shameful lyrics*: Individuals and society risk degradation through music that glorifies egotistical behavior and the abuse of others.

- *Extremely unhealthy foods*: It's okay to indulge once in a while, but should individuals ever be encouraged to eat a fast-food sandwich consisting of bacon and cheese between two deep-fried chicken patties?

- *Risqué restaurants*: Eateries where waitresses are hired based on their physiques objectify the women who serve and disgrace the patrons who visit.

- *Bad bunny*: This final example is very specific and rather random, but hopefully it captures the range of similarly crude products: a plastic rabbit that dispenses jelly beans through its hind quarters.

Non-Denigrating Influence

My fear in sharing the preceding examples and in outlining this chapter's earlier discussion is that readers might get the mistaken impression that all or most of marketing produces a denigrating influence. My contention is just the opposite: the vast majority of marketing influence is positive and profitable for individuals and organizations on both sides of the exchange. In the spirit of balancing the presentation, therefore, I wish to highlight a few examples of non-denigrating influence.

It's important to emphasize that not all marketing allusions to sex are crude or gratuitous, or objectify people. In fact, some references to sex are quite appropriate. Consider, for example, a tropical resort that specializes in honeymoon vacations. It would be fitting for the resort to use a print ad featuring a young man and woman on the beach in bathing suits. It also would be fitting for the ad copy to contain some tasteful reference to intimacy, which is a special part of honeymoons. God created humankind as sexual beings and gave men and women the gift of sex, to be used in the right context. It is appropriate, therefore, for organizations to tastefully market products that support God-honoring human sexuality.

> *Not all marketing allusions to sex are crude or gratuitous, or objectify people. In fact, some references to sex are quite appropriate.*

By the same token, there are many legitimate attention-getting elements that are used in marketing promotion that are not denigrating. A print advertisement, for instance, might grab attention through use of a vibrant color, an intriguing caption, the illusion of movement, or a unique image. There are plenty of examples of marketing that are both highly creative and very effective that do not resort to tasteless measures. Many of us buy groceries at supermarkets that offer value-priced, good-quality products at times and places that are convenient for us. And, the stores promote their offerings through forthright and helpful advertisements (newspaper flyers) and sales promotion (coupons).

Likewise, unlike the car-kissing example, not all promotional contests denigrate consumers. Many are fun and worthwhile for everyone who participates, not just the winners. Our son has taken part several times in a drawing contest sponsored by a well-known company. He hasn't won the contest (yet!), but he's enjoyed the process and produced some really creative pictures that have made him and his parents proud.

Finally, there's nothing wrong with humor in marketing, whether it involves promotion or the product itself, provided that the wit is in good taste and doesn't compromise marketing objectives.

One of the main reasons marketing often endures an undeserved negative reputation is because of the denigrating tactics of unprincipled individuals. Their behavior not only demeans consumers, it also disparages the entire discipline. This analysis of denigration might serve as a step toward reforming such practices, bringing them in-line with the positive influence that marketing most often exerts.

> **Influence Tip #4**: To avoid denigration, show other people the same level of respect that you would like to be shown, and treat the belongings of others (tangible and intangible) as if they were your own valued possessions.

Reflection Questions – Denigration

1. Why do people denigrate other people and things?

2. Do Christians have any special motivation to not denigrate?

3. Are there certain types of humor that are, or are not, denigrating?

4. What specific marketing tactics do you think are most denigrating? Why?

5. What specific marketing tactics have you witnessed that seemed to go out of their way to convey honor and respect? Are such tactics effective?

Chapter 7
FIFTH SIN: INTRUSION

There is a pleasure in the pathless woods,
There is a rapture on the lonely shore,
There is society, where none intrudes,
By the deep sea, and music in its roars:
I love not man the less, but nature more.

—George Gordon Byron

It was a crisp afternoon in late October. Our family had moved just two weeks earlier into a new house. We were still in the throes of unpacking and getting settled into our home. [Note to self: When employed in higher education, the middle of the fall semester is not the best time to move.] Meanwhile, my sister stopped by for a brief visit. This wasn't an ideal time to have guests; however, we were very glad to see her family—they live in Florida and rarely have an opportunity to travel north to Pennsylvania, where our extended family is from. So, en route to my parents' home, they came to see us for a few hours.

As the time of the visit sped by and neared an end, the doorbell rang.

Representative: "Hello. I'm glad I finally found you at home. I've been trying to get to see you."
Me: "Oh?"
Representative: "I'm with Greetings Guild."
Me: "Oh."

Representative: "I have lots of coupons, special offers, and information from great local businesses I'd like to share with you. Is this a good time?"

Me: "Actually, we have some family visiting right now, and they're only here for a short time . . ."

Representative: "Don't worry, it won't take long."

Me: "Yes, but they need to leave soon . . ."

Representative: [stepping inside] "That's fine; I can do this very quickly."

Me: "Well, I suppose . . ."

Representative: "Great." [walking into the living room and settling in for his presentation]

In case you haven't noticed through the first six chapters of this book, I'm a big fan of marketing. I like doing marketing, teaching marketing, reading about marketing, observing marketing, and talking about marketing. Even as a diehard supporter of the discipline, however, I'll be among the first to agree that there are inappropriate times and places for marketing. Such is true for just about everything in life, even the "good" things. Hard work honors God, but not when it unnecessarily keeps you from being a part of your daughter's tenth birthday party. Likewise, it's great to give your spouse a passionate kiss, but not during a funeral service. A key to much of life is knowing to do the right thing at the right time. Marketing is no exception.

> *A key to much of life is knowing to do the right thing at the right time. Marketing is no exception.*

So why was Greetings Guild's representative's visit inappropriate? First, I want to emphasize that in most respects the visit was fine, even desirable. People who move to new areas often need to find quality grocery stores, reliable mechanics, and good dentists. Organizations like Greetings Guild (not its real name) help new residents in their search for such products and services, saving people time and money. In other words, Greetings Guild facilitates mutually beneficial exchange. There was also nothing inherently wrong with the place of the visit. Given that these items are household purchases, it's fitting that they are discussed with consumers in their homes. In contrast, it would be inappropriate for such meetings to occur in consumers' places of work, disrupting their job responsibilities at their employers' expense.

What made the representative's visit intrusive was the insistence on meeting despite signals that doing so would usurp irreplaceable family time. In this particular instance, familial relations and marketing goals were not compatible. As a result, the former should have taken priority over the latter. In defense of the Greetings Guild representative's decision, intrusion is a mistake that many of us readily make in our professional and personal lives. When we don't listen carefully to what others are telling us, verbally or visually, it's easy to slip into the delusion that our agendas are paramount and everyone else's activities are expendable. As a father, husband, and former employer, I know from experience.

Intrusion Described

What is intrusion? *Intrusion* is entering another person's physical or mental space without the other's complete welcome. The location is often a tangible place, like one's home or office, but it also can be a psychological space involving one's thoughts or feelings. Either way, intrusion results in an invasion of a personal privacy. As human beings we often establish boundaries, tangible or intangible, that put limits on our social interaction. Intrusion occurs when marketers cross the boundaries and enter areas of our lives to which we have not fully invited them.

> *Intrusion* is entering another person's physical or mental space without the other's complete welcome.

Of course, what represents intrusion for one consumer may not seem intrusive to another. We all have different likes, dislikes, and degrees of tolerance. While many people treat calls from telemarketers with contempt, some individuals relish the social interaction, even with a complete stranger. Still, virtually everyone needs some physical or mental space to which they can retreat in order to rest, contemplate, or refresh without the distraction of undesired outside influence.

Intrusion is not *just* individual-specific; it's also dictated by the situation. That is, the same person may hold a different perspective on what's intrusive based on the circumstances, or context. My experience with Greetings Guild is a good example of situational influence. Under normal circumstances I would be very open to hearing about the local businesses and receiving some money-saving discounts or other special offers. However, given my unique family situation at the time, the Greetings Guild visit felt like an intrusion into my physical space, and even more an invasion of my emotional space: as I sat on the couch, listening begrudgingly to the presentation, I couldn't help but think, "I wonder what my family is doing now; I should be spending this time with them."

Intrusion in the Bible

As has been the case with many of the other "Seven Sins," intrusion is not a word that is common to scripture. The Bible *does* address the concept, however, through the use of several related terms and ideas which often focus on the positive value that is to be upheld: privacy. Paul urges believers not to be "gossips" or "busybodies," but rather to avoid prying into the personal affairs of others (I Timothy 5:13). Similarly, Proverbs 11:13 extols the virtue of keeping another person's secret while condemning the act of betraying another's confidence.

The Bible also supports the notion that we, as human beings, need some personal space. Proverbs 27:14 says, "If a man loudly blesses his neighbor early in the morning, it will be taken as a curse"—kind of like a neighbor ringing our doorbell at 5:00 am just to wish us a great day. Sure, at some level we appreciate the goodwill, but overwhelmingly we resent the invasion of our privacy (i.e., our mental state of sleep) for a less-than-compelling reason. Even something that is normally good can be taken as an affront if it intrudes on our physical or emotional space.

Perhaps the best illustration of the need to uphold personal privacy comes from Jesus' own example. Despite that fact that the Son of God loves everyone, even he sometimes needed time alone: "Yet the news about him spread all the more, so that crowds of people came to hear him and to be healed of their sicknesses. But Jesus often withdrew to lonely places and prayed" (Luke 5:15-16). Why would God the Son need to go anywhere in order to talk with God the Father? I believe this passage suggests that Jesus' humanity presented some of the same physical and emotional challenges that we experience. Fatigue due to constant travel, teaching, and healing may have threatened his fellowship with the Father. Part of Jesus' regimen for refreshment, therefore, was to temporarily draw away from others

> Despite that fact that the Son of God loves everyone, even he sometimes needed time alone.

so he could commune with the Father and renew himself without distraction. Of course, it's doubtful that Jesus ever referred to anyone's interruption to his solace as intrusion; still, I believe his precedent supports the necessity of occasional personal privacy.

An even more forceful indictment of intrusion comes from a well-known Bible passage and another example in Jesus' life. Matthew 21:12-13 describes how Jesus entered the temple area and proceeded to drive out the merchants who were changing money and selling doves. Some people have used this passage to condemn business, which I believe is a gross misinterpretation. There's no evidence in scripture that Jesus ever took similar action against merchants or that he had a general disdain for business. In fact, as mentioned in Chapter One, there's good reason to believe that Jesus himself was involved in some form of marketing related to his work as a carpenter (Mark 6:3). A more logical interpretation of the Matthew passage is that Jesus was acting against the intrusion of business into a very sacred space. Provided that they were conducted fairly and *outside* the bounds of the Temple, it's unlikely that the same types of commercial activities would have stirred Jesus' righteous indignation. On the other hand, I can envision Jesus becoming just as angry if people were having banquets, playing games, or doing other things in the Temple that weren't specifically about worshiping God. Commerce was not the issue. The problem was that business had intruded into a place where neither it nor a host of other activities belonged.

Intrusion in Marketing

Given that the Bible spurns intrusion, the next step is to identify specific examples of marketing activities that constitute intrusion. Unfortunately, there's no shortage of illustrations. One increasingly common way that some organizations intrude is in the collection and sharing of personal information, which the digital age has greatly facilitated. For instance, a consumer is visiting an internet retailer's website and looking at a particular product when a message appears, indicating that a friend of hers has purchased the same item. At first she's surprised and thinks, "Well, that's a coincidence." After further reflection she begins to wonder how the retailer would have known that she and the other person were friends. The consumer then realizes that the online social network to which they're both connected must have shared information with the retailer.

In keeping with the earlier notion that what constitutes intrusion is specific to the individual, the consumer's response may take one of three main turns: 1) Appreciation: "What a great idea. I hope I'll receive similar messages about other friends' purchases." 2) Indifference: "Well, that's different." 3) Resentment: "It's really inappropriate for those companies to share our personal information. I wonder what purchases of mine they've told my friends about. There may be things I don't want others to know."

The third response reflects the feeling that the organizations' behavior is intrusive, not in a physical sense, but in a psychological way. In publicizing what many people deem to be private behavior (i.e., their online purchases), the firms have crossed into the realm of individuals' privileged thoughts and feelings. It's one thing for a business to record and use data from its own consumers' purchases. We wouldn't expect a firm to neglect or "forget" that information; in fact, we expect that behavior. It's another thing, however, for an organization to share their consumers' information with other firms, and it's a further step to disclose that consumption behavior to its customers' friends. In the latter case especially, it's not hard to imagine how a person could feel emotionally violated: "The things I buy are between me and the business. I'm not ashamed of what I purchase, but I want to be the one who decides who, if anyone, knows what I buy."

What complicates this discussion is that many times firms do secure their consumers' permission to share purchase behavior. The way that consent is obtained, however, often leaves much to be desired. Most of us can empathize with the experience: It's 11:30 pm, and you've just downloaded the latest version of the social network software. You'd like to use it for a least a few minutes before heading to bed, but before you can begin, you need to check a box to indicate that you "have read and agree to the terms and condition of use." You click on the link to do so and a new window opens. For some reason, all of the text is in upper case, singled space, with no indentations or paragraph breaks. You start to read the first paragraph and quickly realize that the agreement is laden with legal-ese that a good attorney would be challenged to decipher. Still, you plod on through the first page, second page, and onto the third page. You stop and ask yourself, "How much longer is this thing?" Using the scroll bar, you move to the bottom of the document and realize it's twenty-one pages. "Even if I stay up and read all of this, I probably won't understand it." So you rationalize that there's nothing detrimental to you in the agreement, you close the window and click the "I agree" button, not giving the document a second thought.

Is it prudent for us to shortcut legal agreements in this way? Of course not. My suspicion, however, is that many, many consumers feel compelled to do so by the length of the documents and inscrutability of the text. If this hunch is correct, then it seems there should be changes to preclude such overwhelming license agreements, which would serve to limit the ability of organizations to intrude.

In keeping with the preceding discussion, there are many ways that the personal information of consumers can be collected. Sometimes firms simply ask for information such as birthdays or evening telephone numbers and consumers willingly comply. Other times the information is gleaned through less conspicuous means. If a client happens to use his cellphone to call a salespersons' cellphone, the salesperson now has the client's cellphone number by virtue of the call log. The potential for intrusion arises, then, based on what the salesperson does with the number once he has it. Using the cellphone number to return the client's call, during normal business hours, may not be intrusive. On the other hand, calling the client's cellphone on a Sunday night to clarify an item on a bid request probably is intrusive.

Of course, the timing of a potentially intrusive act is just one consideration. As Jesus' example in the Temple illustrated, location is another key determinant of intrusion. There are some places where marketing activities should rarely or never occur. I had the opportunity to visit one such place recently: the concentration camp at Dachau. This site was the Nazi's first concentration camp in Germany and the place where thousands of people were wrongfully imprisoned and lost their lives (*Holocaust History: Dachau*, 2011). On such a solemn and somber site, it is appropriate that there are no souvenir shops or other places on the grounds to purchase Dachau memorabilia. That type of retail activity would represent physical and emotional intrusion to visitors who wish to witness the camp in its historic form and contemplate the suffering that occurred there.

Places of special natural beauty represent another set of locations where marketing activities should be restricted or prohibited. Many people take great pleasure in lying on a pristine, secluded beach or hiking an unspoiled mountain trail. These experiences can be much different, however, if banner planes buzz over the beach or billboards line the trail. That kind of marketing promotion can detract from the natural beauty and intrude upon individuals' enjoyment of those places in their pure and unadulterated forms.

Finally, the Church is the place where all Christians should be sensitive to marketing activities. I should preface this discussion by clarifying that what I'm referring to here is *not* marketing *by* the Church but marketing *in* the Church. I believe that there is considerable need for the former; that is, the Church can and should use marketing concepts to support the fulfillment of its mission in much the same way that the Church should use principles from sociology, finance, and nutrition to facilitate its ministries. God has given individuals in the Church knowledge and skills in these and other areas; the Church should use those talents to further His kingdom.

What I want to focus on here is marketing *in* the Church, which for me is marketing that is unrelated to the Church's mission. Within many churches there are individuals whose occupations involve selling directly to other consumers products such as health and beauty aids, cleaning supplies, and kitchen items—useful products that benefit most us. Although it's completely acceptable for Church members to be involved in the marketing of these products, it's not appropriate for that marketing to occur within the bounds of the Church. For instance, the teacher of an adult Sunday school class shouldn't approach a class member afterward to ask if she's interested in buying cosmetics. Similarly, an insurance agent who attends the church shouldn't use its directory to identify new client prospects. Such behavior seems to use the Church as a means to an end. Utilizing godliness as a "means to financial gain" (I Timothy 6:4) is first an issue between the individual marketer and God. Secondly, however, these marketing activities intrude upon the worship and fellowship of other believers. A church should be a place where individuals can freely nurture their relationships with God and others. The use of the church as a venue for business dealings represents intrusion into those important spiritual priorities. More in-depth discussion of Marketing and the Church comes in Chapter Ten.

Non-Intrusive Influence

Despite the numerous examples discussed above, it's important to emphasize that marketing intrusion is the exception, not the rule. When one considers the valuable impact most marketing has on our lives, ranging from the food we buy to the homes we live in, it's apparent that the net effect of marketing is overwhelmingly positive. In the spirit of that collective benefit, therefore, I will highlight three specific examples of "non-intrusion:"

- *Commercial Radio, Television, and Internet:* Although we may not resonate with every ad that airs, when we tune-in to commercial radio, television, or internet we should expect to hear and see advertising; it's what makes those types of media possible. We can't rightly consider that kind of advertising intrusive, unless it intrudes in some unexpected, psychological way, such as by ambushing us with images that are offensive or shocking.

- *Collection of Personal Information:* Is it always intrusive for organizations to gather personal information? I don't believe so, provided that the collection process demonstrates informed consent; that is, customers are fully aware of the data gathered and its purpose, and they willingly agree to share those facts. Furthermore, when the information is shared in an interpersonal context, it is fitting for there to be a measure of *quid pro quo*. For example, if in conversation a salesperson asks a client the ages of his children, the salesperson should offer back the same information, if applicable. A free and balanced exchange of information does not characterize intrusion; it represents natural conversation and encourages relationship-building, which is beneficial to both parties.

- *After Hours Contact:* One of the above examples of intrusion suggested that it was inappropriate to call a client during the weekend. Does this case mean that it is always intrusive to contact customers after business hours? No. As a retail consumer, I appreciate receiving evening and weekend emails from businesses I patronize that include special offers or that inform me of upcoming sales. In a business-to-business context, the circumstances surrounding the communication are especially important. For instance, a client whose rush order failed to arrive Friday as expected will likely appreciate a call that evening, letting her know that the order will be delivered the next morning in time for his company's Saturday afternoon event. Under different circumstances the call is probably intrusive, but in this situation the call helps the client sleep much better that night.

One of my favorite Bible passages is the third chapter of Ecclesiastes, which begins, "There is a time for everything, and a season for every activity under heaven" (Ecclesiastes 3:1). As the passage suggests, building is a great thing, but we can't build continually; at some point we must cease construction and tear down (verse 3). Similarly, it's wonderful to laugh, but it's not always appropriate to do so; sometimes we need to weep (verse 4). I believe there is a fitting parallel here for marketing. At its core, marketing's facilitation of mutually beneficial exchange is a good thing from which we benefit daily. There are times and places, however, where marketing activities can become intrusive, particularly in light of individual preferences and unique situations. It's essential for marketers to recognize this potential and to limit marketing to its rightful place "under heaven."

> **Influence Tip #5**: To avoid intrusion, recognize that there are inappropriate times and places for most things in life, and if in doubt, ask permission.

Reflection Questions – Intrusion

1. Why do some marketers intrude?

2. Is it possible to intrude even if one is initially welcomed and if so, how?

3. How did Jesus model the need to respect privacy–the opposite of intrusion?

4. What specific marketing tactics do you find most intrusive? Why?

5. In what places should there not be marketing?

Chapter 8
SIXTH SIN: ENCOURAGING OVERINDULGENCE

There are limits to self-indulgence, none to restraint.

—Mahatma Gandhi

Cailyn scurried about the kitchen, hurrying to prepare dinner. "All this cooking and baking is hard work," she thought, "but the food isn't going to make itself." She glanced at the clock. "5:15 already?" Connor would be home from work in fifteen minutes. It was times like these that she really appreciated all of the amenities and conveniences of their new house. Settling into a new home is never easy, but for Cailyn and Connor, the change had been well worth it. They loved everything about their house, as they should, given that virtually every detail was customized for them. From the recessed lighting, to the bay window, to the grand staircase, the entire interior was the product of the finest craftsmanship. A professional interior designer had carefully chosen and coordinated all of the home's furnishings, window treatments, and decorative accents to fit their tastes—comfortably plush by any standard.

Connor glanced at the dash of his black Mercedes convertible—5:20 pm. Since he was just over ten minutes from home, he allowed his foot to become a little heavier on gas—not speeding, just making some time so Cailyn wouldn't have to wait for him. Of course, there was no question that his "ride" could handle much more than he was asking.

Four-wheel disc brakes and rack-and-pinion steering were just garnishes on this plate of fine German engineering. Connor navigated a few hairpin turns, then accelerated down a straightaway toward home.

"Okay . . . 5:31 and everything is . . . done." Cailyn muttered these words to herself as she placed the last serving dish on the table. A moment later Connor sped up to the house. Although he was a minute late, he couldn't help but slow, almost to a stop, in front of their home. He admired the fine woodwork on the wraparound porch, the two-story spire, and the flower boxes overflowing with colorful petunias and pansies. It's beautiful, he thought.

As he entered the house, Cailyn was still standing near the kitchen table. "It's good to be home," Connor said.

Cailyn smiled and nodded in agreement. "I hope you're hungry," she urged.

"I sure am," he replied. Just then, a strong, familiar voice echoed from outside: "Connor and Cailyn, dinner time."

"Okay, just a minute, Mom," they responded in unison. The brother and sister quickly turned off the lights of their exquisite playhouse, closed the front door, and raced across the lawn and into their family's full-size house.

What's wrong with driving a Mercedes and living in a nice house?" Nothing, perhaps, if you're an adult. Connor and Cailyn, however, are children, and their car and house are real, kid-size toys. Both items were featured a few years ago in the catalog of a well-known toy retailer. The "Child-Size Mercedes 500 SL," (87" x 40" x 30") came with a gasoline engine, fiberglass body, and full suspension, and sold for $15,000. "La Petite Maison Custom Playhouse," had 8-foot ceilings, running water, and options for heating and air conditioning, in addition to the other features mentioned above. The playhouse listed for "$30,000 and up, depending on size, design, and features selected." Some of the other catalog copy read, "Move up to what may be the most luxurious playhouse in the world . . . When children are used to living well, they should play like this . . . ."

As much as parents love their children and as easy as it is for some families to afford very expensive gifts, should any ten-year-old be the recipient of a $15,000 car or a $30,000 playhouse? Probably not. These items may well be the "poster children" for overindulgence. Parents who buy their kids such extravagant toys are likely guilty of spoiling their children, which is probably a gross understatement. By producing and selling these items, the toy manufacturers and retailer also might be considered accomplices to the overindulgence. In other words, the marketers themselves are not guilty of overindulgence, but it seems they should bear at least some responsibility for encouraging it.

Encouraging Overindulgence—Described

What exactly is *overindulgence*? Overindulgence is *consumption beyond what's beneficial for a person physically, emotionally, financially, or otherwise.* Through typical marketing exchanges, consumers experience net gains in utility. Overindulgence, however, presses the principle of marginal utility beyond its reasonable bounds. A person who likes chocolate and is hungry for something sweet might eat a chocolate bar. If he enjoyed it and is still hungry, he may eat another. As he starts a third bar, the chocolate continues to taste good, though not as great as it did the first or second time. Plus, he is starting to feel full. Still, he finishes the bar. He then proceeds to eat a fourth bar, and a fifth. Now he feels sick and the thought of eating another chocolate bar is completely unappealing. Somewhere in the process the consumer overindulged: he pushed his consumption of chocolate to the point where the negative effects of eating it outweighed the benefits he received.

Of course it's relatively easy to tell when we overindulge on food, at least when the gluttony occurs in a single sitting—our stomachs ache, our pants grow tight, etc. Although excessive consumption is just as possible for many other products, it's often not as readily discernable. Unbeknownst to us we might overindulge on entertainment, clothing, or even something as commendable as education, as when an individual pursues graduate degree after graduate degree in lieu of getting a job. In this case, the marginal benefits of learning one more discipline are eclipsed by the cost of unemployment. The individual may not recognize her overindulgence, however, if the negative outcomes are absorbed by parents who continue to pay for schooling and other expenses.

Overindulgence in the Bible

It's not surprising to find that scripture takes a firm stance against overindulgence. After all, Jesus often taught others to deny themselves in order to follow him (Matthew 16:24; Mark 8:34; Luke 9:23). Likewise, Paul urged believers to put the needs of others ahead of their own (1 Corinthians 10:24, Philippians 2:3-4). Both of these directives stand in stark contrast to self-indulgence. There also are a variety of other passages, however, that seem to offer even more direct condemnation of overindulgence. Some of these passages use the word "self-indulgence." James 5:1-6 denounces the exploitative and self-indulgent practices of the rich, and Jesus rebukes the Pharisees for their self-indulgence, hypocrisy, and greed in Matthew 23:25-26. Certain Bible passages warn against specific types of overindulgence, such as gluttony (Proverbs 23:1-3), drunkenness (Ephesians 5:18), and avarice (Proverbs 23:4-5).

The Bible doesn't just repudiate overindulgence, however. It also demands that believers exhibit what might be viewed as the complete opposite characteristic: self-control. Scripture describes self-control as a means of staying spiritually alert (1 Thessalonians 5:6) and avoiding "ungodliness and worldly passions" (Titus 2:11-14). The Bible also identifies self-control as one of the nine "fruits of the Spirit," alongside the likes of love, joy, peace, and patience (Galatians 5:22-23). When done in excess, even a good behavior can lead to harmful overindulgence, as Proverbs 25:16 warns: "If you find honey, eat just enough—too much of it, and you will vomit." The solution, instead, is to live a life of self-control and not be "mastered by anything" (1 Corinthians 6: 12).

Although the Bible appears to stand against *overindulgence*, it doesn't deny indulgence altogether. God created humankind with needs for at least several basic material things: food, water, clothing, shelter. Of course, all of these things can be consumed in their most rudimentary form—no frills. Certain Bible passages, however, seem to suggest some leniency. For instance, John 2:1-11 describes the wedding ceremony in Galilee that Jesus and his disciples attended. As suggested by Jesus' first miracle, turning the water into wine, the associated banquet must have seen the guests participate in at least some atypical, indulgent behavior. It also may be worth noting that Jesus chose to create a wine that tasted superior to what the guests had been drinking. In addition, people at various times questioned why Jesus took an apparently more liberal approach to "eating and drinking" than did the more ascetic John the Baptist (Matthew 11:18-19; Luke 7:33-34). Did a sinless Jesus ever overindulge? Certainly not. The preceding examples from Christ's life, however, might suggest that carefully controlled and limited indulgence is sometimes acceptable. Still, the overriding point remains that the Bible opposes overindulgence.

> Although the Bible appears to stand against <u>overindulgence</u>, it doesn't deny indulgence altogether.

The Role of Encouragement

It is important to reiterate here that the choice of words *encouraging overindulgence* is very intentional in two specific ways. It is significant that the behavior is *overindulgence* rather than just *indulgence*. Overindulgence is by definition injurious, at least in a minor way, if not more substantially. Indulgence, however, is not necessarily harmful; some limited indulgence is often fine. Eating a rich dessert might be indulgent, but doing so only once in a while may have some intangible value and probably is not overindulgent. Eating a rich dessert several times a day, every day, however, turns nominal indulgence into overindulgence.

Second, given the focus of this chapter, it is essential that the behavior under investigation is *encouraging* overindulgence, not just overindulgence. It sounds axiomatic, but consumers are the ones who consume products, not marketers. As consumers, we hold primary responsibility for our own consumption decisions, provided that marketing influence is free from other improper influence such as deception, coercion, and manipulation. Our decision to overindulge, therefore, is principally our own choice and responsibility. Still, it seems that marketers should at least be held somewhat accountable if they *encourage* the overindulgence of consumers. A key question, therefore, is "What constitutes encouragement?"

In general terms, to encourage is to influence, or persuade. Persuasion, however, can function across a broad range of intensity. The specific words and actions that have persuasive effect may vary greatly depending on the individual and the situation. One might consider dieting, for example. For some people, the only persuasion they need to begin to diet is an off-the-cuff comment from someone they know, such as: "You look different." Other individuals, however, will not start to diet short of a full medical examination, supporting data (high blood pressure, etc.), and an urgent plea from their physician: "You have to lose weight." Given this extreme variation, it's very challenging to specify exactly what constitutes persuasion, or encouragement, particularly in a marketing context in which each consumer is unique and many consumers are exposed to different levels of influence, even from the same marketer.

> *As consumers, we hold primary responsibility for our own consumption decisions, provided that marketing influence is free from other improper influence.*

Biblical Encouragement

As might be expected, the Bible presents encouragement as a good thing, provided it is free from other sinful behavior (e.g., deception and coercion) and it is focused toward an acceptable end. For example, Paul exhorts believers to exercise their gift of encouragement, along with other spiritual gifts such as teaching, giving, leading, and serving (Romans 12:6-8). Paul also recognizes personally the potential that encouragement has to build up others (1 Thessalonians 5:10-11), as he himself offers encouragement in many of his letters (Ephesians 6:22; Colossians 4:8; 1 Thessalonians 4:18).

So, although encouraging others toward spiritual maturity is certainly desirable, not every aim of encouragement is acceptable, particularly if the outcome is sin. For instance, Malachi rebukes priests who have caused the Israelites to sin, or "stumble" in their spiritual walks (Malachi 2:8). Similarly, Paul urges more mature believers to do nothing to cause their less-experienced counterparts to stumble (Romans 14:20; 1 Corinthians 10:32). In addition, Jesus uses the vivid image of a person thrown into the sea with a large millstone tied to his neck, in order to dissuade anyone who might lead others to sin (Matthew 18:6). From the messages contained in these passages, it seems reasonable to conclude that encouraging a sinful act like overindulgence runs contrary to biblical teaching.

Determining Encouragement

Despite the complexity of encouragement and the challenge of its measurement, marketers' relative accountability for consumer overindulgence still can be addressed. In fact, there are specific ways of estimating the extent to which marketing influence encourages excessive consumption. Following are eight questions that might be used to make such a determination. Taken together and applied to a specific consumption situation, the answers to these questions might serve to confirm or contest a marketer's purported encouragement.

1. Are non-marketing factors unlikely to be encouraging overindulgence?

2. Is the overindulgence widespread among members of the market?
3. Are the market's consumers particularly prone to overindulge?
4. Are the market's consumers especially susceptible to marketing influence?
5. Do members of the target market have difficulty affording the product?
6. Does one-time consumption of the product represent overindulgence?
7. Does the product have addictive properties or non-satiating tendencies?
8. Do specific marketing tactics explicitly promote overindulgence?

While a "yes" answer to a particular question suggests that a marketer bears at least some responsibility for encouraging overindulgence, a "no" response places accountability more squarely on the consumer. Each question will now be considered in order.

Q #1: Are Non-Marketing Factors Unlikely to be Encouraging Overindulgence?

One way to think about a marketer's potential complicity in consumers' overindulgence is through the metaphor of regression analysis. One can think of overindulgence as the dependent variable—the main factor of interest that will increase or decrease based on the impact of a series of related factors, or independent variables. Based on my experience with regression, it is unusual for a single independent variable to explain most of the variation in the dependent variable. For example, in a regression model for "winning the Super Bowl" (dependent variable), it's unlikely that one factor alone, such as a "strong quarterback" (independent variable), would explain the victories. Instead, there would probably be many predictive factors (e.g., solid defense, good coaching, accurate kicker, etc.) that each painted a partial picture of why teams have won the championship. Ultimately, after a regression analysis has been run, one can see which specific independent variables were statistically significant predictors and exactly how much of the dependent factor's variation each explained.

In most consumption cases there are many non-marketing factors that can help explain consumers' overindulgence. For instance, consumers who stockpile hundreds of pairs of shoes may be swayed to do so by social influences (e.g., reference groups, like friends; opinion leaders, such as celebrities), by an unusual drive for esteem (i.e., owning so many pairs helps them feel better about themselves), or by past experience (e.g., coming from a background of poverty into wealth). The fact that a particular company manufactures and promotes its shoes does play some role in the overindulgence—if no companies made or promoted shoes, overindulging in shoes would be very difficult. At the same time, any one marketer's contribution to the overindulgence may be negligible. People who participate in this form of behavior probably receive encouragement from any number of other sources, such as those mentioned above, so their behavior would continue regardless of the presence or absence of any one marketer.

On the other hand, if consumers' overindulgence cannot be readily attributed to non-marketing factors, such as social and psychological influences, it is much more likely that the marketer bears responsibility, since there are really only two sources of influence: marketing-generated influence and non-marketing influence. Consequently, if it is *unlikely that non-marketing factors are encouraging overindulgence,* then marketing's encouragement is probable.

Q #2: Is the Overindulgence Widespread among Members of the Market?
What about individuals who seem to overindulge on one particular product or brand, such as a person who has a walk-in closet stacked top-to-bottom with Nike sneakers? Do those situations indicate the

marketer's significant encouragement of overindulgence? Not necessarily—the frequency of the behavior among all consumers should be another important consideration. If overindulgence occurs among a high percentage of product/brand users, then perhaps the marketer is enacting significant encouragement of excess. If, however, very few consumers exhibit the behavior, it seems likely that other causal factors, such as the ones described above, are at work in the lives of those particular individuals. After all, if millions of consumers were exposed to specific marketing influence that encouraged overindulgence, it would seem that more than just a few would engage in overindulgent behavior.

This is another case in which the previous regression metaphor may be helpful. A meaningful regression analysis is based on an adequately-sized sample, or in this instance, a substantial number of brand consumers. To focus on the behavior of a few overindulgent consumers, or outliers, and ignore the responsible behavior of the vast majority of customers would seem like poor sample selection. On the other hand, if *the overindulgence is widespread among members of the market*, it is more likely that the marketer in question is encouraging overindulgence.

Q #3: Are the Market's Consumers Particularly Prone to Overindulge?

Continuing the distinction between overindulgent and sensible consumer groups, marketers also should be aware of the market's general propensity for excess. Certain markets may have an across-the-board tendency to overindulge, for example, the young adult male market for beer (Garfield, 2008). Of course, some maintain that it is the responsibility of consumers to recognize and control their own propensity to overindulge and that mass marketers of products like beer cannot be cognizant of each individual consumer's limitations. This argument may work for markets in which cases of overindulgence are anomalies, but when the patterns of behavior are well established and

SIXTH SIN: ENCOURAGING OVERINDULGENCE • 89

it is known that a certain group of consumers tends to overindulge, it seems irresponsible for marketers to target those consumers. To do so is analogous to a sky-diving business targeting people with severe heart conditions—knowingly putting consumers at high risk of very negative outcomes. Consequently, if *the market's consumers are particularly prone to overindulge*, the marketer bears added responsibility for encouraging overindulgence.

Q #4: Are the Market's Consumers Especially Susceptible to Marketing Influence?

Similarly, some consumers may be predisposed to overindulgence because they are generally more susceptible to marketing influence. Children, for instance, often exhibit different levels of understanding of ads than do adults, which may make kids more easily swayed by the advertising messages they encounter (Lawlor and Prothero 2008). Unlike adults watching television commercials, children may not realize that a certain toy cannot fly by itself or that fast food pictured on television tends to look much better than it does at the restaurant. This under-developed sense of marketing influence makes children and others with similar tendencies more vulnerable to the influence. Marketers, therefore, can be held more accountable for encouraging overindulgence when *the market's consumers are especially susceptible to marketing influence*.

Q #5: Do Members of the Target Market have Difficulty Affording the Product?

A final aspect of consumer analysis considers overindulgence from a different perspective: consumers' ability to pay. Unlike cases in which people overindulge by eating too much food, purchasing too lavish a house, or spending too much time watching movies, this perspective on overindulgence focuses less on the amount and nature of the product consumed and more on what a particular individual can reasonably afford. For instance, it is probably not excessive for an executive who earns a six-figure income to spend $40,000 on a vehicle; however, it likely would be overindulgent for someone earning $19,000 a year to purchase the same car. Marketers may promote overindulgence by encouraging consumers to make purchases that are disproportionately large relative to their disposable income.

One of the most prominent examples of this negative influence is the relentless promotion of credit cards to young people. Although many college students have little or no income, some credit card companies aggressively target them (Johannes 2008). A similar example comes from the rent-to-own (RTO) industry, which tends to target low-income adults who would like to make large household purchases. Many members of the target market do not have strong credit and cannot afford to purchase a 50" TV or a sectional sofa outright, so RTO companies offer payment plans that allow consumers to take the items home under agreements to make small monthly payments (Hill, Ramp, and Silver 1998). What is often downplayed, however, is the very high total cost that people end up paying to eventually own the products. People also may not realize that they forfeit their products and all the money they have contributed to-date if they stop making payments before the end of the contract period (Francis 2000; Fried 2001; Leonhardt 2001). Marketers may be held responsible for encouraging overindulgence when they *target consumers who cannot reasonably afford their products.*

Q #6: Does One-Time Consumption of the Product Represent Overindulgence?

Besides considering the individuals who comprise the market, it may be prudent to analyze the products themselves for their tendency to invite overindulgence, which can occur in two main ways. First, some products are so intrinsically excessive that even a single purchase constitutes overindulgence. The extravagant playhouse described above is one such example. In terms of food, one of the best/worst examples of overindulgence is a well-known restaurant chain's Grilled Shrimp and

Bacon Club, which Yahoo Health recognized as the #1 Worst Sandwich in America. The club has 24 grams of saturated fat, 125 grams carbohydrates, and 1,890 calories—the equivalent of seven McDonald's hamburgers (Zinczenko 2011). If *one-time consumption of the product represents overindulgence*, the marketer bears responsibility for encouraging that over-indulgence.

Q #7: Does the Product have Addictive Properties or Non-Satiating Tendencies?

Products that have addictive qualities may predispose people toward overindulgence, not from a single purchase or use but by precipitating a consumptive chain that individuals find difficult to break. Casino games and other forms of gambling represent one of the more obvious examples (Suissa 2011). Similarly, some snack foods and soft drinks seem to have non-satiating qualities: they taste great but they do not fulfill one's hunger or thirst in proportion to the amount one needs to consume in order to feel satisfied, which may lead people to overindulge (Almiron-Roig, Grathwohl, Green, and Erkner 2009). Firms encourage over-indulgence by marketing *products that have addictive properties or non-satiating tendencies*.

Q #8: Do Specific Marketing Tactics Explicitly Promote Overindulgence?

Beyond the product itself, sometimes other tactics within the marketing mix are complicit in encouraging overindulgence. For instance, a firm's pricing policies, such as a high flat-fee, may lead customers to consume more than they should in order to feel like they are getting their money's worth (Just and Wansink 2001). This behavior can occur for many types of products, including subscription-based entertainment (cable TV, movies) and all-you-can-eat restaurants. This latter example brings to mind a personal experience: My wife and I had been married for a couple of years when we took a few days of vacation to a well-known tourist destination. My wife's brother and his wife had recently visited the same place and recommended that we eat at a particular seafood buffet, which they described as expensive but amazing. We took their recommendation and went to the restaurant one evening. The price of the buffet staggered us—it was more than twice the amount we would normally spend on a dinner out. Still, there we were, at the restaurant with the strong recommendation of our family members, so we decided to go for it. The food was very good and the selection was immense. When we reached the point of fullness we looked at each other and said, "We can't stop yet. We haven't eaten close to what we've paid for this meal." So, we kept going. A half-hour later we stumbled out of the restaurant, grimacing in pain and vowing never to eat that much food again.

Similar situations can occur when retailers run special promotions like buy-one get-one free (BOGO), or they offer a large quantity of the same item for a set price. First, it is important to clarify that such promotions are normally fine as they often provide great value to consumers who need to purchase multiple items anyway. The potential for encouraging overindulgence increases, however, in cases in which consumers tend to have no strong need for another very similar item or for so many items of the same general type (Ethridge 2006). For instance, a men's clothing store runs a promotion: "Buy one leather jacket, get the second one free!" Most men probably don't have a strong need for two leather jackets, and it's unlikely that they will just give a leather jacket to someone else. What's more likely is that the men who take advantage of this promotion will rationalize a less-than-compelling need for a second leather jacket. Similarly, a supermarket runs a special: "Five boxes of Yum-Cakes for $10." The ad emphasizes that shoppers must buy five boxes in order to get the sale price for the cupcakes, which normally sell for $3.99 per box. Do some consumers have a legitimate need for this many cupcakes? Yes, some do. One might wonder, though, how many people buy five boxes in order to receive the sale price and then either don't use all of them before they go bad; or worse, they eat many more cupcakes than they should, because they've already purchased them. When *specific marketing tactics explicitly promote overindulgence*, marketers are guilty of encouraging overindulgence.

To demonstrate that a marketer is encouraging overindulgence is a challenging proposition; nevertheless, the preceding analysis has suggested that it is at least somewhat possible to infer responsibility. I've suggested here that the process of doing so begins by objectively and circumspectly considering the unique factors that are part of a given consumption situation. Furthermore, a systematic approach to accomplish such an assessment is to ask the eight questions that the preceding analyses have engendered:

1. Are non-marketing factors unlikely to be encouraging overindulgence?
2. Is the overindulgence widespread among members of the market?
3. Are the market's consumers particularly prone to overindulge?
4. Are the market's consumers especially susceptible to marketing influence?
5. Do members of the target market have difficulty affording the product?
6. Does one-time consumption of the product represent overindulgence?
7. Does the product have addictive properties or non-satiating tendencies?
8. Do specific marketing tactics explicitly promote overindulgence?

Again, the more "yes" responses these questions produce, the more likely it is that the marketer in question is encouraging overindulgence. In some cases, however, only one affirmative response may be needed in order to suggest encouragement of excess (e.g., question #6). Either way, the personal and societal implications of overindulgence make it worth conducting such an analysis.

As suggested above, the overindulgence of consumers is not necessarily evidence that a marketer is encouraging excessive behavior. As consumers, we often *do not* do the things marketers would like us to do—just consider the plethora of failed products. By the same token, we sometimes *do* things that marketers do not want us to do, even when warned not to do them, for example: standing on the very top of a step ladder, or placing a plastic bag over one's head. A strong view of consumer sovereignty, which says to let people consume whatever they want, may be at the root of marketing activities that encourage overindulgence. However, when marketers pursue consumers' welfare and practice the discipline according to its true tenets, the result tends to be mutual benefit, not excessive consumption.

A strong view of consumer sovereignty, which says to let people consume whatever they want, may be at the root of marketing activities that encourage overindulgence.

The addition of new words to our language can provide an interesting window into societal behavior. In 2010, for instance, the *Oxford English Dictionary* added the word *overthink*, suggesting a growing trend of pondering decisions too much (*Time* News Feed 2011). By extension, it is notable that the word *overindulgence* also can be found in most dictionaries while a variety of other "over" words cannot. For instance, my computer software's spellchecker recognizes *overindulging* but tells me there is no such thing as "oversaving" or "overgiving." Overindulgence is a problem in our society that does not appear to be going away. The excessive behavior is not limited to the products we purchase; it also includes many other activities we "consume," such as work, exercise, and leisure. Too much of even a good thing is too much.

As suggested, sometimes overindulgence is a function of marketers encouraging harmful behavior. Other times, responsibility for overindulgence falls squarely on our own shoulders as consumers. Either way, turbulent economic times require marketers to be especially careful *not* to encourage the overindulgence of consumers. To do so can be analogous to overharvesting a species of fish. Yes, the fishing industry might do well in a given year thanks to an excessive harvest, but such unsustainable activity jeopardizes future yields and may even lead to the decimation of a species. In the same way, people who overindulge might not endure as consumers, perhaps because they become overextended financially or because some other harm befalls them. The last thing marketers should want to do is encourage overindulgence that could jeopardize their consumers. Of course, Christian marketers have the added God-given mandate to show their customers the same love and respect they have for themselves (Matthew 12:31).

Influence Tip #6: To avoid encouraging overindulgence, don't provide products that will harm people physically, emotionally, financially, or in other ways if consumed in a reasonable manner.

Reflection Questions – Encouraging Overindulgence

1. Are there any products or services on which it is not possible to overindulge?

2. Should consumers alone be responsible for their overindulgence? Why or why not?

3. Some alcohol ads contain the tagline "Drink responsibly." Does the need to include such a message indicate a product that should not be marketed? Or, are there other products that should include similar suggestions?

4. Is it okay to market products that are luxuries, or indulgences?

5. Of the eight questions for determining the accountability of marketers for encouraging overindulgence, which do you feel are most important? Which are least important?

Chapter 9
SEVENTH SIN: NEGLECT

More business is lost every year through neglect than through
any other cause.

—Jim Cathcart

Salespeople like all of their clients, but Savings First Federal Credit
Union (SFFC) was one of Tim Jones' favorites. It wasn't because of the
amount of money the organization spent with Tim's firm; Tim certainly
had bigger accounts. Tim enjoyed doing business with SFFC because of
his contact at the Credit Union: its President, Harry Smith. Some customers can make salespeople feel like an interruption or even foster a spirit of antagonism ("Us against you"). Such was never the case with Harry.
Despite the power of his position, he was a very gracious and humble
man who treated everyone with respect, both inside and outside SFFC.
Tim's relationship with Harry felt like a friendship. Harry was also an
extremely busy man. SFFC had recently opened two new branches and
was looking to open two more, with Harry spearheading the expansion.
Such was the backdrop for Tim's latest meeting with Harry:

> **Harry:** "Well, hello, Tim. You don't need to wait out there, come
> on in. It's great to see you."
>
> **Tim:** "It's great to see you too. How has your spring been?"
>
> **Harry:** "Wonderful. We're only about two months away from
> opening the new branch on Bristol Pike around the beginning
> of the year."

Tim: "Yes, I've been watching the construction. It looks like a very nice facility."

Harry: "Thank you. Of course, we're going to need some promotional items for that grand opening, but we can talk about that later. We have a more urgent need now."

Tim: "Sure, what is it?"

Harry: "I think I may have mentioned that June 1 is SFFC's twenty-fifth anniversary. Many of our people have worked here for over half that time and some have even been with SFFC for all twenty-five years. Given everyone's hard work and how far we've come, we want to make June 1 a very special anniversary celebration. I'm wondering what items you'd recommend for us: things we can give to our employees and credit union members. I know I should have contacted you earlier; I've been so busy. I realize there's not much time."

Tim's heart sunk. June 1 was just two weeks away. He knew very few imprinted products could be produced on that tight a schedule, and shipping would add even more turnaround time. He also suddenly remembered Harry's request near the end of their last meeting: "And, Tim, please come see me this spring. We're celebrating our twenty-fifth anniversary June 1. We'd like to get some nice items for an event that day."

Harry's kindness and composure made Tim feel even worse. He knew Harry understood that there were few options at this point. Plus, the situation was really Tim's fault. Harry had told Tim about the anniversary and asked him to follow-up, which Tim should have done a month or more earlier. Harry had the right to be upset, but if he was, he wasn't showing it.

Tim: "I am so sorry for not getting together sooner about this. Let's see what we can do to put together some good options for the event."

Neglect Described

There are many unenviable positions in which salespeople can find themselves: dealing with a belligerent prospect, informing a customer that the wrong item was ordered, losing a long-time client to a competitor. None of these situations is necessarily any more unpleasant than the one Tim experienced. What makes his situation particularly painful is that he could have easily avoided it just by doing his job. As a marketer, Tim's overriding goal is to facilitate mutually beneficial exchange. Now, because he neglected his duty to follow-up with his client, the best Tim can expect in this instance is mutually stressful exchange—there will be a lot of extra work and sleepless nights, hoping that the items will arrive on time.

It's easy to think that the way to prevent inappropriate marketing influence is to just avoid doing the wrong thing, which is largely true. Most of this book has supported that perspective: don't deceive, don't coerce, don't manipulate, don't denigrate, don't intrude, and don't encourage overindulgence. These first six sins have all represented sins of commission—you err if you do them. What marketers must recognize, however, is that there are also sins of omission—you err if you don't do them. This dichotomy is not just true for marketing; it applies to influence in general. For instance, "Parent A" provides for all of his children's physical needs (food, clothing, shelter, etc.). He also does drugs in front of his kids and allows them to participate. "Parent B," in contrast, does not encourage any illicit behavior among her young children. In fact, she is seldom home and pays no attention to her kids' health or schooling. Each of these parents is likely to be labeled a "bad influence." Parent A's transgression is a specific sin of commission—promoting drug use. Parent B's offense is a sin of omission—not fulfilling basic responsibilities of a parent. One might say Parent B is guilty of neglect.

> *When marketers fail to fulfill their basic responsibilities to their clients and other stakeholders, marketers also can be deemed guilty of neglect.*

As the preceding example suggests, to *neglect* is to fail to perform a duty. Or, in the context of our discussion of marketing, neglect involves *not providing the influence expected of a competent marketer.* Like parents, marketers are involved in relationships in which others depend on them to faithfully exercise their discipline-specific skills and use their given resources. When marketers fail to fulfill their basic responsibilities to their clients and other stakeholders, marketers also can be deemed guilty of neglect.

Neglect in the Bible

As has been our practice, we want to try to understand a scriptural perspective on neglect. In most of the Bible verses in which the word appears, neglect serves as part of an admonition against specific spiritual oversight or compromise, for instance: "Be careful not to neglect the Levites as long as you live in your land" (Deuteronomy 12:19); "Do not neglect your gift, which was given you through a prophetic message when the body of elders laid their hands on you" (I Timothy 4:14); "But you have neglected the more important matters of the law—justice, mercy and faithfulness. You should have practiced the latter, without neglecting the former" (Matthew 23:23).

> If neglect represents not completing responsibilities at all, or doing them half-heartedly, diligence involves working with fervor to produce excellent outcomes.

Besides the denunciation of spiritual lethargy, the Bible addresses neglect more broadly by describing how individuals *should* work: diligently. In many ways diligence is the polar opposite of neglect. If neglect represents not completing responsibilities at all, or doing them half-heartedly, diligence involves working with fervor to produce excellent outcomes. Many Bible passages encourage diligence, for example: 2 Chronicles 24:13 highlights the diligent work of individuals who "rebuilt the temple of God according to its original design and reinforced it." Proverbs 10:4 and 13:4 respectively counsel: "Lazy hands make a man poor, but diligent hands bring wealth" and "The sluggard craves and gets nothing, but the desires of the diligent are fully satisfied." Likewise, 1 Timothy 4:15 implores: "Be diligent in these matters; give yourself wholly to them, so that everyone may see your progress." Based on such scriptural mandates, one can reason that market-ers are called not just to *do* their work, but to do it *well*, which means working diligently to "the glory of God" (1 Corinthians 10:31).

> *Marketers are called not just to do their work, but to do it well, which means working diligently to "the glory of God" (1 Corinthians 10:31).*

Neglect in Marketing

Again, neglectful marketing practice doesn't mean doing the wrong thing (e.g., deceiving, intruding, etc.); it's about failing to do the *right*, or expected, thing. Given this understanding, there could be a limit-less number of examples of marketing neglect, ranging from failing to target an obvious market segment to not choosing the optimal promo-tional medium. The examples I would like to highlight here are ones with more obvious impact on end-consumers like you and me.

After just deciding to purchase a new electronic device, many of us tire of what seems like an unending stream of follow-up requests: "Would you like to buy a car charger?" "Can I sign you up for the three-year extended warranty?" Although these types of requests can be overdone, many times they're in our best interest as consumers. In fact, we sometimes become irritated or upset if a marketer neglects to ask or remind us of something important. How many parents have lost their composure on Christmas morning upon realizing that the box containing the popular new toy their children have been eagerly antici-pating does not contain batteries? Certainly it is neglectful for the toy manufacturer not to at least print clearly on the front of the box: "Four 'AA' batteries not included."

Another example from the specialty advertising industry may seem rather simple, but it's a real one that also supports the point. When planning a special event, organizations often order balloons custom-imprinted with their logo or other text (Tyler Industries 30th Annual Company Picnic). Many customers don't think, however, that if they're ordering balloons, they probably also should order some tethering device (string, ribbon, sticks, etc.), especially if they're going to fill the balloons with helium and hand them out to people. A salesperson need only forget to ask his balloon-ordering customers about string one time, and he probably won't neglect the question again . . . "Remember those balloons you sold us? It was the morning of the trade show and we didn't have any string, so we had to send someone out to buy some. Why didn't you tell us to order string?"

As mentioned in Chapter Two, organizations and their agents operate from a position of information superiority—they know their industry and its products much better than do most consumers. It's incumbent upon the marketer, therefore, to guide consumers through the exchange, offering them actionable advice. When marketers fail to do so, they can be considered neglectful. Such neglect might also occur in the face of an impending price increase. If the salesperson knows that the price tomorrow will be 20% higher than it is today, she should let her customer know; otherwise he will probably lament: "Why didn't you tell me the price was going up? I was ready to buy." Similarly, sometimes when consumers are looking for a particular product, they'll call a store to see if it is in stock. If the store associate responds "yes," the consumers also expect him to let them know if it's the last one on the shelf, or to offer to hold it for them. Otherwise a customer might drive ten miles only to find that someone else just bought the only remaining item.

The time period after a sale also poses significant potential for neglect. Although marketing is about facilitating mutually beneficial exchange, it doesn't mean that marketing is a purely transactional phenomenon: "Here's your product, thank you for your payment, have a nice life." Facilitating exchange means providing value for customers over an extended period of time, perhaps indefinitely. Marketing isn't about one-time transactions; it's about encouraging exchange *relation-ships*—bonds that consistently deliver value over time.

This philosophy of marketing suggests that a marketer's duty to the customer does not end after the contract has been signed or the credit card has cleared. Marketers bear at least some responsibility for providing service after the sale, which may mean replacing a faulty product, answering questions about assembly, or providing training for use. Of course, all products are different: what's required for proper operation of a heating and air conditioning system is not necessary for a bag of potato chips. Marketers are guilty of neglect, however, when they fail to provide product-appropriate service after the sale.

Non-Neglectful Influence

The preceding discussion has aimed to help identify the kinds of de-ficiencies that constitute marketing neglect. By extension, then, mar-keting that fulfills its multi-faceted responsibility to consumers is not neglectful; although it still might be improper in terms of one of the other Seven Sins. To further delineate the boundaries of marketing neglect, it may be helpful to describe a few other examples that may on the surface seem neglectful, but are not. For instance, it is fine for a firm's sales-people and its advertising *not* to describe sim-ilar product offerings of competitors. Rational consumers know that most television spots are intended to promote one company's product, not an entire industry, and that salespeople are paid to advocate their own organization's products, not those of other companies. People can and should seek out other sources of information.

> *Marketing that fulfills its multi-faceted responsibility to consumers is not neglectful.*

Similarly, it's not neglectful for an advertisement to focus on one particular feature or benefit of a product. There's only so much time in a 30-second radio spot, and there's a limited amount of space in a full-page magazine ad. We as consumers have limited attention spans and abilities to process information.

> *It's relatively easy to recognize when we do the wrong thing . . . it's usually more difficult to realize when we haven't done the right thing.*

Likewise, marketers should not be considered negligent when consumers misuse or abuse products despite being given sufficient instruction or warning. Rational consumers are solely responsible for the outcomes if they eat a half-gallon of premium ice cream every day or if they try to cut their hair with an electric carving knife. As suggested in the previous chapter, marketers' duties to consumers have reasonable bounds.

It's relatively easy to recognize when we do the wrong thing—think of the number of times you've thought to yourself, "Wow, I shouldn't have done that." On the other hand, it's usually more difficult to realize when we haven't done the right thing. Sins of omission tend to be more subtle than sins of commission. Nevertheless, marketers must do their very best to avoid both types of deficiencies related to the influence they wield. To that end, this chapter has sought to paint a clearer picture of the oft-overlooked and underestimated sin of marketing neglect.

Influence Tip #7: To avoid neglect, serve others with the same diligence, enthusiasm, and professionalism that you would want to receive.

Reflection Questions – Neglect

1. How does a marketer avoid being neglectful but also refrain from bothering or pressuring customers?

2. In this digital age in which people have quicker and easier access to information, is marketer neglect less of an issue?

3. Describe a situation in which a marketer neglected you.

4. Do you agree that it's not neglectful for a marketer to refrain from discussing competitors' products? Why or why not?

5. Does neglect deserve to be a sin on the same level as the other six sins of influence?

PART 3:

THE CHURCH, THE WORKPLACE, AND BEYOND

We've discussed the Seven Sins of Influence by considering their biblical bases, seeing how some marketers commit the sins, and identifying how most marketers can, and do, avoid them. We could conclude the discussion now; however, given that this book's target market is primarily Christians interested in marketing, it makes sense to give some special treatment to the two institutions that all Christian marketers have in common: the Church and the workplace. Here's why...

First, as I have suggested repeatedly, the relationship between marketing and Christianity can be challenging to navigate, even when the marketing is physically separated from the Church. What happens, then, when the marketing is being conducted in the Church or by the Church, where there is deep understanding of Christianity but not necessarily great appreciation for marketing? These intricate issues are the focus of Chapter Ten, "Marketing and the Church."

Second, Christians working outside the Church or for organizations that are not specifically Christian-owned and operated often face the opposite dilemma: colleagues who have a great appreciation for marketing but little or no understanding of Christianity. How can Christian marketers explain the reasons for their moral choices to individuals who don't follow the Bible or perhaps even believe in God? Chapter Eleven, "Christians in a Secular Workplace," offers some suggestions for approaching this critical cross-cultural communication.

Finally, we conclude with Chapter Twelve, "A Balanced Perspective," in which I share one of my most formative experiences as a Christian marketer. The chapter also synthesizes much of the preceding discussion and offers two overarching tips for realizing honorable influence.

Chapter 10
MARKETING AND THE CHURCH

Unlike so many, we do not peddle the word of God for profit. On the contrary, in Christ we speak before God with sincerity, like men sent from God.

—2 Corinthians 2:17 (NIV)

It was Sunday morning, their adult fellowship class had just ended, and Kara and Steve were making their way through the hallway toward the sanctuary for the 11:00 am worship service. A job transfer had led the couple and their three children to move to the area about half a year ago, and they had been attending New Covenant Church for the past four months.

Kara: "I'm really enjoying our Sunday school class."

Steve: "Yes, Ben and Rachel do a great job teaching how the Bible is relevant to our lives today."

Kara: "Just a minute, I want to check our mail." Steve stands by as Kara scans the wall of cubbies and locates the family's recently assigned mailbox. She pulls out a small stack of papers.

Steve: "What'd we get?"

Kara: "Some youth group activities for Kyle and Meg. And here's the membership information we asked for."

Steve: "Good . . . What's that?" Steve points to a colorful flyer that appears to be an ad for something.

Kara: "It looks like a brochure for hair and skin care products . . ." Just then someone interrupts the couple's conversation.

Susan: "Hi, Kara. I'm not sure if you remember me—I'm Susan. We met at the potluck dinner last week."

Kara: "Yes, I do. You live in . . . Pikesville, and you sell beauty products."

Susan: "That's right. You have a good memory! Well, I'm sorry to bother you two, but I just wanted to make sure that you got my flyer. I think I put one in your mail box."

Kara: "Is that what this is?"

Susan: "Yes. I also wanted to mention that all cosmetics will be going on sale next week, just in time for the Holidays. How about I give you a call to see what you might be interested in?"

Kara: Caught off guard. "Sure, I guess so . . ."

Susan: "Great; I'll be in touch." Susan walks away, while Kara stands motionless, still processing what just happened.

Steve: "Now there's a motivated salesperson."

Kara: Regaining her thoughts, "I don't know . . . I wasn't expecting to have a conversation like that here in Church."

Steve: "Yeah, or to get a product flyer like this in our Church mailbox."

Kara: "I like Susan, and it's nice to support the work of other Christians, but it doesn't seem right to be buying and selling products like these at Church."

Marketing in the Church

We live in a marketing-saturated society. As such, it's not surprising to see examples of marketing strategies and tactics almost everywhere we turn. Branded products are all around us. As mentioned in the introduction, the average American is the recipient of hundreds, if not thousands, of commercial messages a day. The combined impact of marketing from all organizations is certainly daunting; yet, taken individually, much of this marketing influence is very useful, if not necessary. For instance, it's helpful when manufacturers and retailers let us know where we can buy products we need and for how much.

Still, as Chapter Seven described, the acceptability of specific marketing influence is partly a function of where and when the influence occurs. A commercial message delivered across a conference table during a business meeting might be very appropriate, while the same message shared at a family gathering across the dinner table might be very unwelcomed. The notion of unacceptable times and places for marketing influence was at the heart of the explanation involving the fifth sin—intrusion.

Chapter Seven also identified a number of Bible passages that seem to suggest the inappropriateness of marketing in the Church; that is, individuals bringing their commercial endeavors into God's house for personal benefit. Probably the most poignant biblical admonition of such behavior was Jesus's clearing of the temple of those changing money and selling doves (Matthew 21:12-13). As was discussed, these acts were not necessarily wrong in and of themselves. What prompted Jesus's righteous indignation was likely *where* the selling was being conducted. The Temple was the holiest of places, reserved for the most sacred of activities. When people entered God's house they were to be prepared physically and spiritually. Nothing was to distract them from the all-powerful creator of the universe.

> *A certain commercial message delivered across a conference table during a business meeting might be very appropriate, while the same message shared at a family gathering across the dinner table might be very unwelcomed.*

With the birth of the New Testament Church, worship practices also changed. There were no more sacrifices of crops or animals, and both Jews and Gentiles were welcomed into fellowship. At the same time, a sense of God's holiness and the need to show ultimate respect for Him remained. Paul chided the believers in Corinth for desecrating the Lord's Supper by treating it more as a banquet or party than as an act of sacred remembrance. (1 Corinthians 11:17-22). Likewise, the writer of Hebrews exhorted his readers to "worship God acceptably with reverence and awe" (Hebrews 12:28). From Old to New Testament times, some of the specific practices and places of worship had changed, but God had not. Even today, He still demands that worshipers give Him attention and reverence, particularly when they enter His house.

But can these Bible passages and apparent expectations for sanctity in worship be used to evaluate what happened in the case of Kara and Steve's church experience? After all, our economic and social systems today are very different than they were more than 2,000 years ago. It's true—much has changed since biblical times, but God the Father and Son have not: "Jesus Christ is the same yesterday and today and forever" (Hebrews 13:8). As such, it is not hard to imagine Jesus, in New Covenant Church or another contemporary place of worship, exhorting Susan and others to give their full attention to God and to stop selling their products in His Father's house. Marketing by individuals for personal benefit still does not belong in the Church.

Marketing by the Church

Those reading carefully may have noticed that the previous heading said "Marketing in the Church," while the current one reads "Marketing by the Church." As the saying goes, "What a difference a word makes." More specifically in this case, one small but very important preposition potentially changes everything.

The previous section argued that it is inappropriate for individuals to market products for personal benefit in the Church because God's house is not the place for those activities; rather, its primary purpose is to provide a special venue for worshiping Him. However, the practice of "marketing in the Church" is considerably different than that of "marketing by the Church." In the case of the latter, the question to be answered is whether the Church should itself employ marketing strategies and tactics. Based on the previous discussion, it's understandable for the initial reaction to be "no way." If individuals shouldn't market in the Church, why should the Church be marketing?

The key difference is what's being marketed, or advanced, and why. When individuals market their own products and services to others within the Church, they promote things that may or may not be consistent with the Church's mission, largely for their own benefit, as well as for the benefit of select others—they are primarily advancing their own mission. In another context this marketing may be fine and even desirable; however, within the Church it can distract from or impede the Church's mission, as discussed above. When the Church uses marketing strategies and tactics it usually does what it's supposed to be doing—fulfilling its mission, advancing God's kingdom, and drawing people closer to Him.

> When the Church uses marketing strategies and tactics it usually does what it's supposed to be doing—fulfilling its mission, advancing God's kingdom, drawing people closer to Him.

In a broader context, marketing is one of several business disciplines whose tools can be harnessed for the good of the Church. It behooves every congregation to employ best practices in accounting in order to keep track of its income and expenses, to adhere to sound financial principles in order to effectively manage debt, and to utilize human resource techniques to care for staff. In many ways, marketing represents just another one of these toolsets, which God gave humankind the intellect to create and use. It's reasonable to suggest that God gifted Joseph with skills in administration and planning, which he ultimately used to save his people and countless others from starvation (Genesis 41:46-57). Similar skills also were likely used by Job (Job 1:1-3), Daniel (1:1-7), Boaz (Ruth 2:1-3), and the Wife of Noble Character (Proverbs 31:10-31). Even Jesus, as a carpenter, probably used skills in business and marketing in producing and selling his wares (Mark

6:1-3). Jesus's Parable of the Shrewd Manager, in which he includes the following exhortation, also appears to suggest that business savvy can be used to accomplish God's purposes: "I tell you, use worldly wealth to gain friends for yourselves, so that when it is gone, you will be welcomed into eternal dwellings" (Luke 16:1-9).

Once again, a careful reader may have noticed another very intentional word choice two paragraphs above: "When the Church uses marketing strategies and tactics it *usually* [emphasis added] does what it's supposed to be doing . . . ." Unfortunately, there are ways in which a church's unchecked use of marketing can work against God's desire for believers. As suggested throughout this book, one of marketing's primary goals is to give consumers what they want and need—a concept that's at the heart of creating mutually beneficial exchange. Failure to satisfy its consumers' wants and needs is the ultimate sign of a flawed marketing plan.

Given the marketing-driven society in which we live, it's almost natural for churches to think of current and potential congregants as their consumers. As such, an individual church might seek to adapt its "marketing mix" (product, place, promotion, and price) to most closely match what its attendees want and need. Some of this adaption is desirable, if not necessary. Recognizing that children, young teens, and adults are at different stages in their intellectual and social development, most churches tailor certain programs, like Sunday School classes, to each group's unique needs. Many churches also see worship style as an acceptable area for adaptation and modify their worship services to match the style that feels most comfortable to their congregants (e.g., traditional vs. contemporary worship).

> **If anyone is the Church's consumer it's God.**

Ultimately, however, the purpose of the Church is not to satisfy congregants, but God. He created humankind for His pleasure, to glorify Him, and he made the Church the bride of Christ (Revelation 21:1-9). If anyone is the Church's consumer it's God. Although marketing is about creating mutually beneficial exchange, there's no such guarantee for those who choose to follow Christ. While it's true that "in all things God works for the good of those who love him, who have been called according to his purpose" (Romans 8:28), believers are also charged to deny themselves and take up their cross in following Jesus (Matthew 16:24). Although a certain amount of concern for self may be necessary, a Christian's primary directive is to love God and others (Matthew 19:16-19).

A church misuses marketing when it prioritizes the wants of congregants over the desires of God. There are a variety of things that people might want from their church experience that are inconsistent with what God wants. They may want a worship service that's comfortable and entertaining rather than challenging and edifying. They may prefer socializing instead of serving. They may want to be confirmed rather than be convicted. It can be tempting for any church to cater to superficial consumer desires as doing so is often effective in attracting attendees. Such practices, however, are unfaithful to the Gospel and represent an inappropriate use of marketing.

Notwithstanding the preceding significant concerns, there *is* biblical support for churches to use certain marketing practices. The marketing concept as we know it really didn't exist until the 1950s or 60s (Borden, 1964; Levitt, 1960; Smith, 1956); however, even in the Bible there are examples of practices that illustrate and affirm specific marketing strategies and tactics.

Planning

Every good marketer plans, or sets goals and determines how to accomplish them. In fact, the quintessential marketing document is called a *marketing plan*. Nevertheless, Christians in marketing should ask, "Does God endorse planning?" "Does He want me to plan?" It doesn't take long to find ample biblical support for answering these questions "yes." God demonstrates foresight and orderliness in His instructions for building Noah's ark (Genesis 6), the Tabernacle (Exodus 26), and the Temple (1 Kings 6). God's creation of the universe demonstrates even greater planning (Genesis 1). Furthermore the whole Bible, from Genesis to Revelation, can be seen as God's plan for salvation, with the goal of reconciling humankind to himself.

Segmentation and Targeting

It is God's desire that every person turn to Him (Matthew 18:14). Still, even during biblical times, God used different methods to target specific people groups. One of the best examples of this varied approach is when God called Paul and Barnabas to be "a light for the Gentiles" (Acts 13:44-48). Did this special commission mean that God had given up on his chosen people? No. God still desired to bring Jews into relationship with him. Targeting this group were other individuals, such as the many other apostles who remained in and around Jerusalem and Judea.

Supply Chain Management/Distribution

One of the most important functions of marketing is to get the focal product or service to the right place, at the right time, in a manner that maximizes value for both producer and consumer. Not long after the Israelite's Exodus from Egypt, Moses faced a unique supply chain challenge. He was spreading himself too thin in trying to serve as arbitrator for every dispute in a nation of well over a million people. Moses' father-in-law Jethro recognized the unsustainability of the situation and offered some wise distribution-related advice (Exodus 18:13-26). He instructed Moses to set up a hierarchy of capable judges who would collectively serve as a supply chain for judicial service to groups of "thousands, hundreds, fifties and tens" (v. 21). Apparently the distribution plan worked, allowing Moses to both keep his sanity and satisfy the people's need for justice for the next forty years.

Business-to-Business Marketing

As end-consumers, when we think about marketing we typically envision the types of goods and services that are targeted toward us—business-to-consumer, or B2C marketing. There is, however, another realm of marketing that's even more expansive, which involves businesses marketing their goods and services to other businesses, or B2B. It's notable that the Wife of Noble Character described in the Epilogue of Proverbs "supplies the merchants with sashes," which means she markets products to other businesspeople, making her a business-to-business marketer (Proverbs 31:24). Even more notable, however, is the fact that she is one of very few people in all of scripture who God seems to hold up as a complete role model. All of her behavior, as far as we know it, is laudable. And what is her occupation? She's a marketer!

Personal Selling

Although it's inappropriate to equate commercial communication with spreading the Gospel, there are techniques that appear to be relevant to both, particularly in the realm of personal selling. The Apostle Paul demonstrates selling skills that any good salesperson today would want to emulate: building strong relationships (Acts 20:1-37), adapting one's message to a specific audience (1 Corinthians 9:19-23), and constructing and delivering a persuasive argument (Acts 18:4; Acts 26:1-29). In many ways Paul is a model salesperson. Personal selling also may be the facet of marketing that has a more direct biblical connection than any other. The Bible passage that probably illustrates that relationship most explicitly is "The Great Commission:"

> Then the eleven disciples went to Galilee, to the mountain
> where Jesus had told them to go. When they saw him,
> they worshiped him; but some doubted. Then Jesus came
> to them and said, "All authority in heaven and on earth

> has been given to me. Therefore go and make disciples
> of all nations, baptizing them in the name of the Father
> and of the Son and of the Holy Spirit, and teaching them
> to obey everything I have commanded you. And surely I
> am with you always, to the very end of the age (Matthew
> 28:16-20).

I don't wish to diminish the great significance of this extremely important mandate, but looking at this passage through the lens of marketing, one might say that Jesus was "exhorting his salesforce to get out there and sign some contracts." Or, perhaps even more, he was charging them to recruit other salespeople to the eternal cause.

Of course, Christians often recognize the Great Commission as the primary motivation for evangelism. Other support for sharing the Gospel comes from sources such as the life and teachings of Paul (e.g., Acts 13-28; Ephesians 1) and the examples of other apostles like Peter and John (Acts 4:1-22). Christianity's very rapid spread was largely due to the great duty that earlier believers felt for spreading the good news. Likewise, most of us who call ourselves Christians today can only do so because of God's grace and the willingness of one or more believers to practice the evangelism that touched our lives and led us to believe.

Given incredible advances in technology, as well as significant developments in marketing science over recent decades, it's now easier than ever to communicate a message to individuals across the street and around the world. So, Christians should feel even more empowered to evangelize, right? Apparently many don't feel that way. Barna Group (2013) found that born-again Christian's concern for evangelism has been in decline across almost every major demographic group: Baby Boomers, Busters, and Elders. The only age cohort experiencing an increase in the practice of evangelism is Millennials. Barna suggests two reasons that might explain Millennials' contrarian behavior: 1) they tend to have more passion for social justice than other age cohorts, which might correlate with concern for others' spiritual well-being; 2) compared to other generations, a lower percentage of Millennials identify themselves as born-again and/or evangelical, so those who do may hold an even deeper commitment to their faith.

Regardless of the cause of these trends, there's no reason to think that evangelism is any less important than it was two thousand years ago. People still need to be reconciled to God through Christ. What has changed in the United States and in many other parts of the world, however, is that evangelism must occur within increasingly pluralistic societies that tend to reject the promotion of one set of beliefs over another. Given this context, how might evangelism be effective as we move further into the 21st century, and what role might marketing play? These are difficult questions to answer, but here are three specific ideas that further speak to the Church's potential use of marketing:

> *Social media also can be used to build relationships and to demonstrate how one's life and values are different.*

Social Media

The specific platforms that people use to connect with each other in the virtual or digital realm will continue to change, but it seems that the general social media trend will continue to grow for the foreseeable future. These new media give people unprecedented ways to connect with their friends and others, and any of these virtual venues could be used as tools for evangelism. Christians need to be sensitive, however, to how often they post messages that are explicitly spiritual: just as with other forms of communication, coming on too strong or too often can have the opposite effect on those one is hoping to influence for Christ. Besides more overt witnessing, social media also can be used to build relationships and to demonstrate how one's life and values are different. At the right time, then, opportunities may present themselves for more faith-focused conversation.

Events

Whether it's the Super Bowl or a book signing, events are increasingly important facets of marketing for many organizations. Churches also can use community outreach events as instruments for evangelism. Two different churches to which I've belonged have held "sportsmen's banquets," which are evening or weekend events that include a free dinner with a prominent outdoors theme like hunting, fishing, etc. There also is a speaker who talks about these activities and shares his faith. In the part of the country I'm from, each banquet easily attracts several hundred men, bringing some of them inside a church for the first time in many years, or for the first time ever. There also are at least several men at each banquet who give their life Christ. Using such community-oriented events for purposes of evangelism seems to offer great potential within an increasingly pluralistic society.

Business as Mission

Of course, a key part of Jesus's Great Commission is the idea of traveling outside of one's home territory in order to reach the unreached: "Therefore go and make disciples of all nations . . ." (Matthew 28:19). Some nations today, however, are closed to foreign missionaries and will not grant them visas. Many of these same countries do, though, allow individuals in other occupations to enter, including businesspeople. There's a great opportunity, therefore, for those with business skills to enter these countries, contribute to their economies, and advance God's kingdom through their actions, if not through more direct forms of evangelism (Lai, 2005). Such opportunities underscore the increasing need for those in business and in other lay fields to see their work (what they're paid to do) as an important part of their larger Christian vocations.

To summarize the main points of this chapter, most of the marketing with which we are familiar—the goods and services we regularly consume—does not belong in the Church. There's nothing necessarily wrong with the buying and selling of clothes, cameras, or most other consumer goods, but those transactions don't need to take place in God's house, where they can easily distract us from the Church's main purposes: to worship God and to bring people into closer relationship with Him. At the same time, the Church should feel free to use marketing to help fulfill its own mission—the purposes just mentioned. The Bible offers specific support for the Church's use of many key marketing strategies and tactics, including for purposes of evangelism. There are limits to the use of marketing by churches, however. If the use involves putting congregant's wants ahead of God's desires, that marketing has overstepped its bounds. God is the Church's first and foremost consumer, not us.

Reflection Questions – Marketing and the Church

1. What do you think of individuals conducting marketing for their businesses within the Church? What if they give a percentage of the proceeds to the Church?

2. Jesus cleared the Temple of those changing money and selling doves (Matthew 21:12-13). Is that act relevant to marketing in the Church today? Why or why not?

3. What's the difference between "marketing in the Church" and "marketing by the Church"?

4. To what extent are people the Church's consumers?

5. What are appropriate ways for the Church to use marketing?

Chapter 11
CHRISTIAN ETHICS IN A SECULAR WORKPLACE

To the weak I became weak, to win the weak. I have become all
things to all men so that by all possible means I might save some.
—1 Corinthians 9:22 (NIV)

Five months into his new job, Lucas is loving his work as an account executive for FormFactor, a cutting-edge marketing firm located just outside of Chicago. He enjoys the extensive contact he has with clients, as his work requires him to communicate frequently with them in order to ensure that their marketing needs are being understood and met. Lucas also likes the creative connections in his job. Although he's not personally responsible for designing logos, building websites, or writing ad copy, he appreciates that he has input into all of these things by virtue of his interaction with members of his firm's creative department, as he acts as a liaison between clients and others in his company.

Of course, enjoyable work is often challenging, but this week has brought a unique test for Lucas. One of FormFactor's clients is an indoor rock climbing business called Climbaddict. The company already has three of the largest and nicest facilities in the Chicago area. It's now looking to expand northwest into Madison, WI and southeast in to Fort Wayne, IN. Lucas, who has been Climbaddict's account executive for the past two months, is now tasked with helping pave the way for the company's expansion by building brand awareness in these two new markets. Because Madison and Fort Wayne are "college towns," they both already have a considerable number of well-entrenched competitors in the indoor rock climbing arena, which tends to be a favorite pastime of college students, particularly eighteen- to twenty-five-year-old males. The question, therefore, is how FormFactor can help Climbaddict break into these markets and differentiate itself in the highly competitive rock climbing space.

Members of FormFactor's Strategy Team think they have the solution. They believe they can effectively reach the target market by creating ads that feature what really interests most young men: young women. More specifically, the Team proposes a campaign consisting of a combination of Internet and print ads that contain pictures of minimally attired eighteen- to twenty-one-year-old year-old girls, in provocative poses, on some of Climbaddict's rock walls. These sexually-charged ads, the Team's members say, "will really grab attention and set Climbaddict apart from the competition."

Lucas can't deny that these ads will be attention getting. In fact, he finds himself tempted to leer at the pictures that the Creative Team has begun to collect in preparation for next week's client meeting when he and two of his FormFactor colleagues will pitch the campaign idea to Climbaddict. Yet, he feels unsettled by the sex-based approach. Lucas is a Christian and believes that it's wrong for advertising to use such overly-sexual images. That night he spends some time reading his Bible, looking specifically for passages that deal with lust, causing others to stumble, sexual immorality, and showing respect. Among others, he finds the following verses:

- "You have heard that it was said, 'Do not commit adultery.' But I tell you that anyone who looks at a woman lustfully has already committed adultery with her in his heart" (Matthew 5:27-28).

- "So whether you eat or drink or whatever you do, do it all for the glory of God. Do not cause anyone to stumble, whether Jews, Greeks or the church of God" (1 Corinthians 10:31-32).

- "Flee from sexual immorality. All other sins a man commits are outside his body, but he who sins sexually sins against his own body. Do you not know that your body is a temple of the Holy Spirit, who is in you, whom you have received from God? You are not your own; you were bought at a price. Therefore honor God with your body" (1 Corinthians 6:18-20).

- "Show proper respect to everyone: Love the brotherhood of believers, fear God, honor the king" (1 Peter 2:17).

As Lucas considers these passages and others that reinforce similar themes, he becomes increasingly convinced that the proposed campaign runs contrary to what God would want. He shares his dilemma and feelings with his wife Lara. "It's not right for me as a Christian to take part in running these ads," he says. As a result, he feels compelled to speak up and let others know of his concerns. "They're rational people," he reasons. "They should be able to understand and accept my perspective."

How can Christians marketers act faithfully upon their own beliefs while showing respect for the differing value systems of their colleagues?

Lara agrees: "You're right, Lucas, the Bible does offer many principles that seem to contradict the use of oversexualized advertising. And, I think you're right to take a stand." She then asks her husband a very important question: "Are the people who you'll talk with about this situation Christians?"

Lucas's eyes close and his face tightens as he hears his wife's question and realizes the added challenge he has been trying to rationalize. "No, they're not believers. I think Gene is an atheist, Cindi is agnostic, Aamil is Muslim, and I'm not sure exactly what Reva believes." Even if Lucas's coworkers were Christians, it could be difficult to gain consensus on a sensitive issue like this one, given the situation's complicating factors and individuals' possible different interpretations of scripture. The fact that none of his coworkers reads the Bible makes the likelihood of persuading them to his point of view seem even more improbable. What should Lucas do? Or, more generally, how can Christians in the workplace act faithfully upon their own beliefs while showing respect for the differing value systems of their colleagues?

Ethical Diversity

As Lucas and Lara keenly realize, the United States is an increasingly diverse country, in many different ways. In terms of race, America's portion of White residents, which stood at about 62% in 2014, is expected to decrease to about 44% by 2060. Meanwhile, the combined populations of Asian, Black, and Hispanic residents will total over 50% by the same time (Percentage of Population, 2015). America also continues to become more culturally diverse, including its religious composition. While the U.S. is still "home to more Christians than any other country in the world," the number of Americans who describe themselves as Christians has dropped significantly, from 78.4% in 2007 to 70.6% in 2014. During the same time period, those claiming no religious affiliation increased from 16.1% to 22.8%, and those identifying with non-Christian faiths rose from 4.7% to 5.9% (American's Changing, 2015).

Many different factors can impact the moral sensibilities of individuals, but one's religious commitment certainly is among the biggest influences. Consequently, Christians shouldn't be surprised that fewer and fewer people in the U.S. share the same moral standards that they do, which coincides with a rise in *ethical pluralism:* "the idea that there are many theories about what is 'right' and 'wrong' (moral norms) which may be incompatible and/or incommensurable with [one's] own personal moral norms" (Ethical Pluralism, 2011). As such, the "foreign" moral situation in which contemporary Christians find themselves bears some resemblance to the one that Peter described a couple of thousand years ago:

> Dear friends, I urge you, as aliens and strangers in the world, to abstain from sinful desires, which war against your soul. Live such good lives among the pagans that, though they accuse you of doing wrong, they may see your good deeds and glorify God on the day he visits us. (1 Peter 2:11-12)

As a Christian living in the United States and working in the advertising industry, Lucas is also an "alien" in terms of his ethics, or at least in terms of how he might naturally communicate his moral views. He would like to convince his coworkers at FormFactor that it's wrong to create highly sexualized ads for Climbaddict. However, if he tries to persuade them by quoting scripture or otherwise referencing the Bible as the reason for altering their approach, at best he's likely to receive an apathetic response from individuals who don't see scripture as God's Word. Worse, he might anger one or more of his co-workers if they feel he is proselytizing, or they otherwise resent his appeal to his personal religious moral standards. So, how can Lucas and other marketers act faithfully upon their own beliefs while respecting the different value systems of their colleagues?

Common Ground

Fortunately God's special revelation through scripture is not the only way that people have an understanding of morality. Within every person He created, God has implanted a sense of right and wrong. The Apostle Paul explains:

> The wrath of God is being revealed from heaven against all the godlessness and wickedness of men who suppress the truth by their wickedness, since what may be known about God is plain to them, because God has made it plain to them. For since the creation of the world God's invisible qualities—his eternal power and divine nature—have been clearly seen, being understood from what has been made, so that men are without excuse. (Romans 1:18-20)

It doesn't matter if a person has never read the Bible or even if he/she doesn't believe in God. Because God created human beings in His image (Genesis 1:26-27), all people have an innate sense of the Divine and of His standards of right and wrong. Granted, influences of this world may weaken these predispositions or even overwrite them, but a God-instilled sense of morality exists in everyone to some extent. Evidence of this inborn ethical awareness can be seen in many ways, including through Natural Law, the "system of beliefs supposed to be inherent in human nature and discoverable by reason rather than revelation" (Natural Law, 2015). Why has it been that almost every society since creation has condemned actions such as theft, murder, and rape? It's because God has placed within everyone a moral compass that is guided by reason, patterned after the Divine. Even if people don't recognize God, His ethical imprint is still upon them.

Even if people don't recognize God, His ethical imprint is still upon them.

Evidence of our ingrained morality also can be seen through specific principles that many different religions have embraced. Probably the most significant of these universal morals is the Golden Rule, which commands: Do unto others as you would have them do unto you. In others words, treat people like you want to be treated. What's particularly important to note here is that every one of the world's major religions has a version of this same imperative (Universality of the Golden Rule, 2009), for instance:

- *Christianity:* "So in everything, do to others what you would have them do to you, for this sums up the Law and the Prophets" (Matthew 7:12).

- *Buddhism:* "Hurt not others in ways that you yourself would find hurtful" Udana-Varga 5, 1).

- *Hinduism:* "This is the sum of duty; do naught onto others what you would not have them do unto you" (Mahabharata 5, 1517).

- *Islam:* "No one of you is a believer until he desires for his brother that which he desires for himself" (Sunnah).

- *Judaism:* "What is hateful to you, do not do to your fellowman. This is the entire Law; all the rest is commentary" (Talmud, Shabbat 3id).

How is it that each of these major religions, as well as many others, share the same principle? Did they copy each other? No, it's because God has written His moral laws on the hearts of everyone. Those whose consciences have not been overwritten by some countervailing forces are able to appreciate those principles even if they have no relationship with their creator.

A Flexible Fixed Approach

In a society that is becoming more secular and religiously pluralistic, Christians will find it increasingly difficult to persuade others to their ethical perspectives using the specific language of the Bible and their faith. Fortunately, however, the common moral ground described above provides the foundation for fruitful communication with individuals who have different worldviews. Still, one should follow four biblically-informed guidelines for discussing ethics with others who espouse non-Christian beliefs:

1. Talk in terms of others' beliefs.

When the Apostle Paul was in Athens, he demonstrated his knowledge of the local culture and customs through his carefully chosen remarks in a meeting of the Areopagus:

> Men of Athens! I see that in every way you are very religious. For as I walked around and looked carefully at your objects of worship, I even found an altar with this inscription: TO AN UNKNOWN GOD. Now what you worship as something unknown I am going to proclaim to you. (Acts 17:22-23).

Given his belief in Christ and his background as a devout Jew, Paul was himself a strict monotheist; however, he made a concerted effort to understand the beliefs of his target audience members in order to develop rapport with them, a practice he also describes in 1 Corinthians 9:19-23. Jesus took a similar approach in his teaching, often using parables and other metaphors that involved sheep, which were relevant and accessible to audiences that were very familiar with shepherding (e.g., Matthew 25:31-46; John 10:1-18).

In discussions of ethical issues today, Christians should follow a similar approach of adapting their communication to the language of their target audience members who have different worldviews. Just like someone who is bilingual in English and Spanish should speak in Spanish to Spanish-speakers, Christians should translate their moral rationale into words and concepts that others can more readily understand. This approach doesn't mean that they change or concede their beliefs; rather they simply explain their ethical positions using language that is tailored to their hearers.

For instance, in the opening scenario, Lucas's rationale for not using oversexualized ads is based on a number of Bible passages related to avoiding lust, preventing sexual immorality, not causing others to stumble, and showing respect to others. Although the scriptural support for his position is true and compelling, hearing Bible verses probably will not convince Lucas's non-Christian coworkers. What might persuade them, however, are his arguments translated into concepts that are more familiar to them. For instance, most of business is based on achieving certain results—sales, net income, return on investment. Given this utilitarian tendency, Lucas could explain that although the highly sexual ad content is likely to grab attention, it might overshadow the actual product or service and fail to lead to action, in this case, sales of new memberships. In addition, in a society that's increasingly sensitive to the objectification of women, the ads also are likely to offend many inside and outside the target market, which could result in a backlash against Climbaddict. Furthermore, Climbaddict's positioning vis-à-vis the sexualized ads would be painfully hard to undo if the company later sought to expand its target market to women—a potential path for market development given the increasing interest of women in climbing. Finally, Lucas could appeal to universal moral principles via the Golden Rule by raising the question of whether the sexualized images convey the same level of decency and respect that he and his colleagues would want from others.

Lucas's coworkers would likely find the preceding points persuasive. Equally important, in presenting such rationale to them Lucas would not be compromising his faith-based beliefs; rather he would be translating his rationale into language that others more readily understand and appreciate. In an increasingly secular and pluralistic society, it's very helpful for Christians to be ethically bilingual (Hollinger, 2002, p. 254).

2. Be rational.

Talking in terms that are accessible to others is a rational thing to do. However, Christians' persuasive approach in discussing ethics should extend even further in terms of its rational content. The main point here is that one should appeal primarily to reason, not to emotion. It's true that God created us as emotional beings who experience joy, fear, grief and other sentiments; however, these feelings are not the best guides for our decision-making, particularly for complex issues. In fact, such emotions can easily lead us to take action that does not honor God or respect others.

Thankfully God also created us with amazing minds that have deep intellectual capacity. Our ethical decision making is best served when we use our cognitive abilities to reason in order to identify our moral standards, consider relevant facts, and make appropriate judgments based on the preceding items (Shaw & Barry, 2012). Furthermore, this rational approach tends to resonate with our fellow human beings, who God also created in his image (Genesis 1:26-27) and endowed with the skills to reason right from wrong (Romans 1:18-20) using principles that are evident in the natural order (Natural Law, 2015).

As described above, Paul took such a rational approach in his discussions with the Athenians (Acts 17:22-23) and the Corinthians (1 Corinthians 9:19-23). In addition, Paul often reasoned with others from the scriptures in an effort to bring them to faith in Christ (Acts 17:2; Acts 18:19). Perhaps the most notable recorded example of Paul's reasoning occurred during his trial before King Agrippa (Acts 26:1-29). In any case, Paul's extensive use of rational thought serves as excellent examples for contemporary Christians in their quest to engage in moral reasoning with their non-Christian colleagues.

3. Show sensitivity.

While rationality is very important in ethical decision making, it's also important in these situations to balance sound reasoning with sensitivity to the beliefs and feelings of others. A main reason for showing such sensitivity is that by identifying the issue as a moral one there is almost automatically the implication that someone is acting unethically and, of course, people don't like to be called immoral. How can one navigate such a delicate situation in a sensitive way? One key is the choice of words. In Lucas's situation, it could be easy for him to say something to his coworkers like, "You shouldn't be making those oversexualized ads for Climbaddict." Such an accusatory statement is likely to elicit a defensive and perhaps angry response. It would be better for him to broach the topic by saying something along the lines of the following:

> People don't like to be called immoral.

> I've been thinking about the ads for Climbaddict. They're very creative, and they'll really grab attention. I wonder, though, if we might consider a different approach. More and more people seem to be concerned about the way women are portrayed in ads. Climbaddict could receive some backlash from men and women. Maybe there's an approach we could take that would be just as creative but would avoid any negative PR and also would leave the door open for future campaigns targeting women.

If this response sounds better than the first one, the likely reasons are:

- First-person singular and plural subjects (I/we) are more embracing and less accusatory than "you." They also create the feeling that "we're in this together."

- Giving a compliment shows that the messenger recognizes good work and is not just being critical. It also lessens resistance to the less favorable comments to come.

- Rather than coming across as all-knowing and dogmatic, several word choices show humility, e.g., "I wonder," "people seem," "maybe there's an approach."

- An overall positive framing of the issue focuses attention less on the existing concern and more on how things might be even better. Likewise, while it's good to offer solutions and not just identify problems, it's probably best in this situation for Lucas not to offer a specific prescription for the revised ads. That way he's not overstepping the bounds of his position, rather he's allowing his colleagues, the creative and strategic experts, to lay claim to the solution.

Although the Bible supports that there are times for more direct and less diplomatic language, discussions of ethical issues with nonbelievers are likely a better time to follow the Bible's guidelines for more congenial communication:

- "Be wise in the way you act toward outsiders; make the most of every opportunity. Let your conversation be always full of grace, seasoned with salt, so that you may know how to answer everyone" (Colossians 4:5-6).

- "Then we will no longer be infants, tossed back and forth by the waves, and blown here and there by every wind of teaching and by the cunning and craftiness of men in their deceitful scheming. Instead, speaking the truth in love, we will in all things grow up into him who is the Head, that is, Christ (Ephesians 4:14-15).

Beyond what one says (the content), how one says it is also important, including tone of voice and body language. Readers can find other good resources on these topics, so I won't address them here. However, if there is one meta-principle that can serve as a guide for all communication (content and form, verbal and nonverbal), it's represented in Paul's mandate above to the Ephesians to "speak the truth in love."

4. Obey God rather than men.

We have dealt thus far with the difficult task of engaging in conversations about ethical issues with individuals who do not believe the Bible or have a Christian worldview. The central premise has been that it's possible to reach agreement with such colleagues if one gains understanding of the others' perspectives and is willing to adapt his/her communication in order to invite consensus. What happens, though, if unanimity is unattainable and the differing perspectives cannot be bridged?

First, one should seek validation that the position supported is in agreement with scripture and appears consistent with God's will. If these criteria can be verified, it's likely that one will need to stand his/her moral ground and hold to biblical principles in the face of countervailing perspectives. In other words, follow the example of Peter and the other

> If there is one meta-principle that can serve as a guide for all communication . . . it's represented in Paul's mandate above to the Ephesians to "speak the truth in love."

apostles and "obey God rather than men" (Acts 5:29). Christian marketers should have ethical outlooks that are capable of flexing, but ultimately their morality must be anchored in what God deems honorable influence.

Reflection Questions – Christian Ethics in a Secular Workplace

1. How have you seen "ethical diversity" in your place of work, school, etc.?

2. Is it becoming harder for Christians to find acceptance for their moral points of view? Why or why not?

3. What moral heritage do Christians, people of other faiths, and individuals with no spiritual commitment share?

4. Is it right for Christians to translate their moral convictions into language that non-Christians might more readily understand and accept? Why or why not?

5. What are appropriate roles for reason and emotion in discussion of ethical issues?

Chapter 12
A BALANCED PERSPECTIVE

> We come into this world head first and go out feet first; in
> between, it is all a matter of balance.
>
> —Paul Boese

It was a brisk March evening. The College's auditorium was packed—full of students, faculty, staff, administrators, and members of the local community. All had come for the presentation of an internationally acclaimed media critic and documentary filmmaker who was the keynote speaker for a week-long humanities symposium. I sat in the middle of the crowd, eager to hear what she would say about the topic: "The Cultural Manipulation of Community and Belonging: Advertising and Addiction."

As might be expected, the presentation was very polished and professional: a stream of poignant analyses carefully choreographed with an array of impactful slides, most of full-color magazine ads. What I didn't expect, however, was the one-sidedness of the critique. Example after example of presumably malevolent promotion soon produced the underlying message that advertising was an absolute evil with no redeeming value.

I couldn't believe what I was hearing. Certainly some ads deserved censure for being deceitful, sexually explicit, or otherwise reckless, but to give the impression that these relatively isolated instances represented the whole of the field seemed very irresponsible. I had worked in two sectors of advertising for almost ten years. I knew such a wholesale denunciation of the discipline was untrue and unfair, based on my business background, as well as my experience as a consumer.

The formal part of the presentation ended and the question and answer time began. Although I wanted to speak up, I felt intimidated. The room was sprinkled with brilliant Ph.D.'s and full professors from a variety of disciplines, some of whom probably held business in low regard. I, in contrast, was a young Instructor in Marketing with only a few years of experience in higher education and still working on my doctorate. Who was I to publicly question an internationally renowned speaker and guest of our college? In the meantime, several others had raised their voices, praising or otherwise validating the presentation. Still, I felt compelled to speak. I watched my hand go up, which caught the speaker's attention; she acknowledged my intent. Swallowing hard and struggling to control my nervousness, I uttered:

Me: "Thank you for coming. I've appreciated your analysis and agree that certain advertisements pose serious concerns for our society."

Speaker: "Yes, thank you."

Me: "I also have a question. I recently purchased a new car. The main reason I bought it was because of a television commercial I saw. The ad mentioned that the vehicle had a 10-year/100,000 mile warranty, which was very appealing to me because I tend to worry about big repairs. I'm still very satisfied with the car. I'm also very appreciative of that ad; without it, I wouldn't have known to buy the vehicle. My question is this: Is all advertising as destructive as the examples we've seen tonight?"

The example and question seemed to catch the speaker off-guard. She hesitated a little then responded by saying that many local ads are fine. She asked if the ad I had seen was a local ad. I replied that it wasn't; it was a national ad. This response appeared to cause her to stumble slightly before she uttered something about not all national ads being destructive. I thanked her for her response. The evening ended and everyone went their way. As quickly as people moved from the auditorium, most probably also forgot about the details of the presentation. I, however, couldn't shake them from my mind. I kept thinking of how the speaker had painted an extremely narrow and negative picture of advertising and how, by extension, she had misrepresented and maligned the discipline of marketing. Many of my colleagues from across campus had attended the presentation, as had many of our department's students. I couldn't allow either group to hold that evening's lecture as their lasting impression of marketing, so I decided to do something. I wrote the following response and posted it on our college's Community of Educators list-serve:

Subject: Truth About Advertising
A Response to the Kilbourne Lecture

I commend the School of the Humanities for bringing Dr. Jean Kilbourne, a nationally known lecturer, author, and consumer advocate, to our campus on March 10. Dr. Kilbourne aptly identified several important social concerns related to the negative influence of certain types of advertising. For example, some advertising portrays women in ways that treat them as objects. In addition, there is much more advertising than most of us would like for products such as cigarettes and alcohol. Also, ads for these specific products often do make blatantly false associations, e.g., healthy people smoke cigarettes.

It was unfortunate, however, that Dr. Kilbourne's portrayal of advertising was so one-sided. I cannot recall a single slide that served as a positive example of advertising, nor do I recollect a single mention of a redeeming aspect of the discipline. As a result, the not-so-subtle inference from the lecture was that all advertising is destructive to society. This interpretation of the lecture represents not only my own view but also those of others with whom I've spoken. In fact, one of the comments that compelled me to write this response came from an advisee and student of mine who, after attending the lecture, thought she should no longer be a marketing major.

Let me reiterate that Dr. Kilbourne did effectively and accurately identify several critical problems for which some advertisers must be held accountable. I also will add that I have spoken with other people who appreciated many aspects of Dr. Kilbourne's presentation. Ultimately, however, I feel that her lecture propagated an undeserved, negative stereotype of all advertising, which undermines possible reform. The balance of my response highlights specific concerns related to the methods Dr. Kilbourne employed and the informational content she shared during her presentation.

In my classes, I have discussed several of the following methods that Dr. Kilbourne used, which researchers and lecturers generally try to avoid. First, it's easy to find literature or other evidence to support almost any position, so one should strive for an objective portrayal and not selectively choose information. Some support for this criticism of the lecture was given above; more will follow.

In addition, one should maintain clear separation between disparate issues, being careful not to mix them, which obscures arguments and misleads listeners. Throughout her lecture, Dr. Kilbourne repeatedly alternated between discussions of questionable advertising approaches (e.g., use of sexuality) and destructive products (e.g., beer). The methods that some advertisers use and the products that some ads portray represent two distinct issues. It's easy, however, to make the approach used to advertise a sweater appear questionable when that ad is showcased between an ad for Marlboros and another for Absolut Vodka.

Finally, researchers are trained to be cautious about generalizing their findings. A sample should be representative if generalizations are to be made from it to the larger population. I have been a student of marketing (the broader discipline that encompasses advertising) for many years, and I am currently studying at the doctoral level. I also have worked in areas of advertising for about ten years. In addition, I am a consumer who, like most, encounters countless promotional messages each day. Despite this intentional and chance exposure to many advertisements, I recognized only a few of the ads Dr. Kilbourne shared. Her inference was that one could generalize from these few ads to all advertising. Anecdotal evidence, however, suggests that her sample ads are not representative of the entire population of advertising.

Beyond some dubious methods, however, the foremost criticism of Dr. Kilbourne's presentation stems from what might be considered biased content. I will focus on three inaccuracies. First, Dr. Kilbourne presented an uncharacteristically narrow view of advertising. Based upon the look of most of the ads (full-color, glossy) and her comments, it seemed that the vast majority of Dr. Kilbourne's ads were taken from national magazines, and most appeared to be those of for-profit companies. Admittedly, these types of ads are a significant portion of all advertising, yet according to any statistics that I have read, these types of ads are far from the majority of advertising.

In keeping with this allegation of narrow focus, I do not believe Dr. Kilbourne offered a definition or meaningful description of the presentation's main construct—advertising (a formal identification of key terms is a good idea for any lecture). Advertising is commonly considered to be any form of mass communication that is paid for by an identified sponsor (Lamb, Hair, & McDaniel, 2004). Advertising, therefore, encompasses regional and local promotions, as well as national ones; it includes a variety of media such as radio, television, newspapers, billboards and other signage, the Internet, brochures, flyers, and direct mail; and, it is used by all types of organizations including colleges, hospitals, government, social agencies, and churches. It is hard to imagine that advertising done in all of these forms and by all of these types of organizations is as categorically offensive as Dr. Kilbourne's presentation purported.

A second major flaw involved a misrepresentation of the marketing concept. Marketing is the process by which a seller encourages a buyer to participate in a mutually beneficial exchange of products, services, or ideas. The marketing concept refers to the seller's desire to satisfy the wants and needs of the buyer by strategically altering elements of the marketing mix, which are often labeled product, place, promotion, and price. The promotion variables involve ways in which the seller communicates with the buyer; advertising is one of those means of communication. Dr. Kilbourne misrepresented the marketing concept as she showed advertisements from trade publications that talked about delivering certain target markets to prospective advertisers. Certainly, some of the metaphors these ads used were in poor taste (e.g., forwarding a bag of eyeballs).

On the other hand, one must question whether advertisements should be scrutinized for using some of the same benign humor and figures of speech that most of us use in our own daily communication. For instance, I've often heard people speak about acquiring a "headcount" for a luncheon or a meeting, but no one objects to this morbid-sounding talk. The industry expression "delivering a target market" may sound impersonal to those outside of marketing, but properly interpreted the phrase reflects a strategy that is consistent with the marketing concept and that is in the best interest of consumers.

By identifying a specific group of people who are most likely to benefit from a firm's product (i.e., selecting a target market), and by tailoring the product and related elements to the unique needs of those individuals, the firm greatly improves the likelihood of meeting consumers' needs and of creating a win-win outcome. Advertising that is well-written and properly targeted, therefore, often receives a warm reception from consumers who are thankful for the information they receive, which allows them to purchase and benefit from products that they otherwise may not have been aware of—such is a true representation of the marketing concept. Personally, I am grateful that last year I saw a national television ad for a car that I otherwise would not have considered purchasing. I bought the car and have been very satisfied with it. I don't feel that I was manipulated, and I don't want my money back. I think the advertiser of the vehicle benefited; I know I did. My suspicion is that most consumers can identify many of their own such positive experiences with advertising.

Finally, Dr. Kilbourne purported that advertising is responsible for several social ills. As previously discussed, one first should be careful to distinguish certain types of harmful ads (ones that employ particular questionable tactics or those that promote specific destructive products) from the rest of advertising. Furthermore, in any research, one should be cautious about ascribing causality. Eating disorders represent a devastating social problem that we all would like to see eradicated. Do ads that show inordinately skinny models actually cause eating disorders, however? My instincts tell me that certain ads definitely cannot be helping the situation. At the same time, though, one should not overlook other influential factors such as Americans' taste for high-calorie foods, aversion to regular exercise, and obsession with physical appearance. Although I am not willing to do so, one could tender a rather extreme argument that reverses the causal chain and contends that American's obsession with thinness leads advertisers, who want to meet consumers' needs and expectations, to choose emaciated models for their promotions. Continuing this reasoning, many have argued that advertising is more a mirror of society's values than it is a molder of those values (e.g., Lantos, 1987; Pollay, 1986). It also may be fair to ask, why would advertisers want to conspire to create a society of gaunt consumers? If anything, one might speculate that such collusion would seek an opposite goal—to create a norm that favors larger consumers, who conceivably might demand more products and/or bigger ones. Again, let me say that I am not willing to absolve advertising of all responsibility related to eating disorders or to the other social problems that Dr. Kilbourne mentioned. I believe, however, that inaccurately or prematurely concluding that advertising is the principal cause of these problems may serve to discourage much needed research into other factors that are perhaps even more influential.

The advertising industry, like many fields, contains practices that cry out for reform. There is no question in my mind, however, that advertising as a whole serves many useful purposes both for the organizations that advertise and for the consumers who benefit from the products, services, and ideas that are advertised responsibly. There is nothing inherently wrong with paid-for mass communication. It is wrong, however, to forfeit objectivity and balance and to negatively stereotype an entire industry and group of people. Such a one-sided approach is likely to erect barriers to meaningful dialogue and estrange those in the advertising industry who have the power to turn recommended reforms into reality. I hope that certain advertising practices will be changed. I also hope that we will promote a balanced perception of advertising so that my advisee and other people of integrity will be encouraged to enter the field, not leave it, and in doing so, help bring about specific reforms where they are needed.

A Charge to Readers

That evening in March was a turning point for me in understanding the highly polarized perspectives that exist on marketing influence. I had come from a career as a business practitioner where there was little discussion of marketing doing anything wrong. Now I was working in academia where some seemed to believe that marketing couldn't be trusted to do anything right. I realized like never before that neither of these extreme views was valid: marketing certainly is not innately evil, nor are all activities performed under the name of the discipline beyond reproach. Since that time, it has been a primary goal of mine to help bridge the divide by offering a *balanced perspective* on the discipline. Such has been an overarching theme of this book. I now offer this view as a specific charge to readers: identify positive *and* negative practices in the field and speak out, as I've tried to do, on *both* accounts.

For example, don't fall silent when others claim that all marketing is bad. Remind them in a caring and tactful way of the full scope of the discipline. It's not just advertising, but also includes product development, distribution, service after the sale, and more. You also might help them appreciate the many ways that the marketing efforts of a wide variety of organizations benefit them daily (the food they eat; the clothes they wear; the books they read). By the same token, don't fall silent when others suggest or excuse marketing practices that employ one or more of the Seven Sins. Tell a coworker that a tactic your firm is looking to employ seems manipulative, or let a retail manager know you felt deceived by the way a product was portrayed in the store's advertisement. Don't concede to either extreme perspective of marketing.

> *I had come from a career as a business practitioner where there was little discussion of marketing doing anything wrong. Now I was working in academia where some seemed to believe that marketing couldn't be trusted to do anything right.*

By necessity much of this book has focused mainly on what not to do, detailing specific behaviors that individuals and organizations involved in marketing should avoid. Deception, coercion, manipulation, denigration, intrusion, encouragement of overindulgence, and neglect—if marketers can circumvent these Seven Sins while practicing their discipline, they will likely achieve influence that both honors God and appropriately influences people. Along the way, this discussion of "don'ts" has inferred at least two universal "dos," or guiding principles for all behavior. These principles may be particularly helpful in complex cases, when it's difficult to discern whether or not one of the Seven Sins is at work. Here are the two principles with an example to illustrate each:

1. *Influence others to their benefit.* Gerald takes his car to the repair shop to get two new front tires. In the process of installing the tires, the mechanic sees that the front brake pads are worn precariously thin. He tells Gerald about the pads and asks if he can replace them. When Gerald declines, the mechanic continues to describe the severity of the situation and the potential danger that exists. Is this additional urging coercive? Probably not. Even if Gerald is feeling pressure to comply, that pressure is for his own good, as well as that of other drivers, if Gerald's car cannot stop in time. Marketing influence that works to consumers' benefit, not their detriment, is appropriate and honorable influence.

2. *"Love your neighbor as yourself"* (Luke 10:27). The creative director of a large advertising agency is overseeing a campaign proposal for a potential new client. Her firm would love to win the account, which would represent a major increase in revenue for the agency. The client has told all agencies vying for the work that it is looking for something new and exciting. The manager's team executes an oceanside photo shoot involving attractive young male and female models. The resulting pictures are highly creative. They are also very sexually-charged due to the models' scant clothing and suggestive poses. The creative director reviews the photos and asks herself if she would want her children to be pictured in these ways or if she would want other family members to be exposed to these images

as they flip through the pages of their favorite magazines. Her answer is "no," and her decision is to identify a different creative approach. When marketers are in doubt as to whether their influence will be positive or negative, the Golden Rule is an invaluable guide. Ask yourself if, as a consumer, you would welcome the influence. If you can honestly and objectively say "yes," then the influence is probably appropriate and honorable.

To have the opportunity to influence others is both a fantastic privilege and an awesome responsibility. Individuals and organizations that practice marketing are continually exercising influence. It is their duty to ensure that they wield this privilege responsibly. At the same time, it is the duty of consumers not just to hold marketers accountable, but to be fair partners in the exchange and to acknowledge the benefits that accrue to them and to society through proper practice of the discipline. Illegitimate marketing practices can do considerable harm, but a proper approach to the discipline can help accomplish extraordinary good economically, socially, and even spiritually. If consumers and marketers share an informed and balanced perspective of what marketing is and how it should function, it is likely that the marketing activities we all experience will exhibit the best forms of honorable influence.

> *To have the opportunity to influence others is both a fantastic privilege and an awesome responsibility.*

Reflection Questions – A Balanced Perspective

1. What do you think of the author's interaction with Dr. Kilbourne during her presentation and his written response afterward? Should he have responded differently?

2. Is it right for an individual to present a one-sided view of a topic? Does the subject make a difference, e.g., healthy eating vs. automobile safety vs. child pornography?

3. To what extent does it seem to you that views of marketing are polarized, i.e., people either maintain that the field is completely good, or they contend that it's entirely bad?

4. Why does it matter if people who are not marketers have a poor impression of the discipline?

5. Is it possible for marketers to follow the book's final recommendations to "influence others to their benefit" and to "love your neighbor as yourself"? Why or why not?

REFERENCES

About AMA: Definition of Marketing (2013). Retrieved July 30, 2013 from the American Marketing Association website: https://www.ama.org/AboutAMA/Pages/Definition-of-Marketing.aspx

Almiron-Roig, E., Grathwohl, D., Green, H., & Erkner, A. (2009). Impact of some isoenergetic snacks on satiety and next meal intake in healthy adults. *Journal of Human Nutrition and Dietetics, 22 (5),* 469-474.

America's Changing Religious Landscape (2015, May 12). *Pew Research Center.* Retrieved July 28, 2015 from PewForum.org website: http://www.pewforum.org/2015/05/12/americas-changing-religious-landscape/

Barna Group (2013). Retrieved February 14, 2015 from the Barna Group website: https://www.barna.org/barna-update/faith-spirituality/648-is-evangelism-going-out-of-style#.VN-r7ebF-So

Borden, N. H. (1964). The concept of the marketing mix. *Journal of Advertising Research,* 2-7.

Brown, K. & Wiese, M. (2013). *Work that matters: Bridging the divide between work and worship.* Lexington, KY: Emeth Press/Aldersgate Press.

Ethical Pluralism (2011). *EIESEL Project.* Retrieved July 28, 2015 from Ethicsofisl website: http://ethicsofisl.ubc.ca/?page_id=180

Ethridge, M. (2006, June 10). 10 for $10? Don't Buy More Than You Need - Is it a deal? Do the math: Pricing strategy confusing, but we have tips for consumers. *Akron Beacon Journal.* D1.

Francis T. (2000, September 27). Rent-a-Center grabs the stage as expansion drive pares debt. *The New York Times,* T2.

Fried, J. P. (2001, August 23). Rent-a-Center charged with price gouging. *The New York Times,* B8.

FTC Guides (2009, October 5). FTC publishes final guides governing endorsements, testimonials. *Federal Trade Commission.* Retrieved October 24, 2015 from FTC website: https://www.ftc.gov/news-events/press-releases/2009/10/ ftc-publishes-final-guides-governing-endorsements-testimonials

FTC Policy (1983, October 14). FTC policy statement on deception. *Federal Trade Commission.* Retrieved March 9, 2016 from FTC website: https://www.ftc. gov/public-statements/1983/10/ftc-policy-statement-deception

Garfield, B (2008, April 8). Young males are out to get drunk, not pay it forward. *Advertising Age, 79,* 146.

Hagenbuch, D. J. (2008). Marketing as a Christian vocation: Called to reconciliation. *Christian Scholars Review, 48,* 83-96.

Hawkins, D. I. & Mothersbaugh, D. L. (2010). *Consumer behavior,* 11th ed. New York: McGraw-Hill/Irwin.

Hill, Alexander. (2008). *Just business: Christian ethics for the marketplace, 2nd ed.* Downers Grove, IL: InterVarsity Press.

Hill, R. P., Ramp, D. L., & Silver, L. (1998). The rent-to-own industry and pricing disclosure tactics. *Journal of Public Policy & Marketing, 17,* 3-10.

Hollinger, D. P. (2002). *Choosing the good: Christian ethics in a complex world*. Grand Rapids, MI: Baker Academic.

Holocaust History: Dachau (2011). Retrieved February 18, 2011 from the United States Holocaust Memorial Museum website: http://www.ushmm.org/wlc/en/article. php?ModuleId=10005214

Honesty/Ethics in Professions (2014, December). *Gallup*. Retrieved May 30, 2015 from Gallup.com website: http://www.gallup.com/poll/1654/honesty-ethics-professions.aspx

Hunt, S. D. (2002). *Foundations of marketing theory: Toward a general theory*. Armonk, NY: M.E. Sharpe.

Informed Consent Law & Legal Definition (2015). Retrieved July 30 2015 from USLegal website: http://definitions.uslegal.com/i/informed-consent/

Johannes, A. (2008, August). College bound. *Promo, 21,* 22-24.

Johnson, S. (2016, September 29). New research sheds light on daily ad exposures. *SJ Insights*. Retrieved March 8, 2016 from SJ Insights website: http://sjin-sights.net/2014/09/29/new-research-sheds-light-on-daily-ad-exposures/

Just, D. R. & Wansink, B. (2011). The flat-rate pricing paradox: Conflicting effects of "all-you-can-eat" buffet pricing. *Review of Economics & Statistics, 93,* 193-200.

Lai, P. (2005). *Tentmaking: The life and work of business as missions*. Colorado Springs, CO: Authentic Publishing.

Lamb, C. W. Jr., Hair, J. F. Jr., & McDaniel, C. (2004). *Marketing*, 7th ed., Cincinnati, OH: South-Western College Publishing.

Lamb, C. W. Jr., Hair, J. F. Jr., & McDaniel, C. (2010). *Marketing*, 11th ed. Mason, OH: South-Western Cengage Learning.

Lantos, G. P. (1987). Advertising: Looking Glass or Molder of the Masses? *Journal of Public Policy & Marketing, 6*,104-128.

Lawlor, M. A. & Prothero, A. (2008). Exploring children's understanding of television advertising: Beyond the advertiser's perspective. *European Journal of Marketing, 42,* 1203-1223.

Leonhardt, D. (2001, December 16). TV's, DVD's: All yours, but first do the math. *The New York Times,* 4.

Levitt, T. (1960). Marketing myopia. *Harvard Business Review, 38,* 45-56.

Lustig, B. (Producer), Molen, G. R. (Producer), & Spielberg, S. (Producer/ Director). (1995). *Schindler's list* [Motion picture]. Universal City, CA: Universal Studios.

Magrath, A. J. (1986). When marketing services, 4 Ps are not enough. *Business Horizons, 29,* 44-50.

Matear, M. & Dacin, P. A. (2010). Marketing and societal welfare: A multiple stakeholder approach. *Journal of Business Research, 63,* 1173-1178.

Natural Law (2015). *The Free Dictionary.* Retrieved on July 28, 2015 from theFreeDictionary.com website: http://www.thefreedictionary.com/natural+law

Parisi, T. (2015, April 22). The big picture: NIU's Heide Fehrenbach explores history of humanitarian photography. *The NUI Newsroom.* Retrieved March 8, 2016 from http://newsroom.niu.edu/2015/04/22/the-big-picture/

Percentage of Population in the United States as of 2014, by Ethnicities (2015). *Statista*. Retrieved July 28, 2015 from Statista.com website: http://www.statista.com/statistics/270272/percentage-of-us-population-by-ethnicities/

Pollay, R. (1986). The distorted mirror: Reflections on the unintended consequences of advertising. *Journal of Marketing, 50,* 18-36.

Quoteland.com search (2016). Retrieved March 8, 2015 from Quoteland website: http://www.quoteland. com/search.asp

Saad, L. (2015, December 21). Americans' faith in honesty, ethics of police rebounds. *Gallup*. Retrieved March 8, 2016 from Gallup.com website: http://www.gallup.com/poll/187874/americans-faith-honesty-ethics-police-rebounds.aspx?g_source=rate%20the%20honesty%20and%20ethical%20standards&g_medium=search&g_campaign=tiles

Shaw, W. & Barry, V. (2012). *Moral Issues in Business*. 12th ed. Stamford, CT: Wadsworth, Inc.

Smith, J. W. (2016). *Choice Behavior Insights*. Retrieved March 8, 2016 from CBI website: http://cbi.hhcc.com/writing/the-myth-of-5000-ads/

Smith, W. R. (1956). Product differentiation and market segmentation as alternative marketing strategies. *Journal of Marketing, 21,* 3-8.

Suissa, A. J. (2011). Vulnerability and gambling addiction: Psychosocial benchmarks and avenues for intervention. *International Journal of Mental Health & Addiction, 9,* 12-23.

Time News Feed (2011). New words in the OED. Retrieved February 12, 2011, from http://newsfeed.time.com/new-words-in-the-ode/

Universality of the Golden Rule (2009). *TeachingValues.com*. Retrieved July 28, 2015, from http://www.teachingvalues.com/goldenrule.html

Violet, J. (2007, October 13). Car kissing contest—This got my lips salivating. FemaleFirst. Retrieved September 4, 2010, from http://www.femalefirst. co.uk/ motoring/motornews/motoring-1403.html

Zinczenko, D. (2011). Worst sandwiches in America. *Yahoo Health*. Retrieved January 25, 2011, from http://health.yahoo.net/experts/eatthis/ worst-sandwiches-america

APPENDIX

David Hagenbuch wrote the following article, which was published in 2008 in Christian Scholars Review, 48, 83-96, and is reprinted here with the journal's permission.

MARKETING AS A CHRISTIAN VOCATION: CALLED TO RECONCILIATION

In titling this paper "Marketing as a Christian Vocation," I was struck by the notion that for many other disciplines, a similar choice of words would be much less controversial. For instance, would people be as skeptical of an article entitled "Social Work as a Christian Calling" or "Nursing as a Christian Vocation"? This question is not meant to suggest that these disciplines are uninteresting or not conducive to Christian service. In fact, the implication is exactly the opposite: To a great extent, people seem to accept these and many other fields as ones in which people readily do work that is honoring to God. Marketing, however, enjoys few such positive associations.

Indeed, for some, to associate marketing with Christian vocation represents something between paradox and blasphemy, analogous to "Money Laundering as a Christian Calling," or "Pirating Software for Jesus." A teaching colleague of mine, for example, once bantered, "Your class is called Marketing Principles? Isn't that an oxymoron?" Also, during a sermon I heard a few years ago, the speaker remarked matter-of-factly, "Advertising is lying." Even in an introduction to marketing textbook, a case study mentioned in passing that car salesmen are "the most untrustworthy people." These isolated comments are not particularly troubling; however, when considered along with numerous works that have documented negative perceptions of marketing,[1] the collective implications should be of concern to Christians in higher education. Marketing is a major at a large number of Christian colleges and universities, yet students often seem to be the recipients of a conflicting message that marketing is not an acceptable field in which to serve God. The tragedy of this miscommunication is that our world greatly needs individuals to practice marketing in a way that is true to the discipline's theoretical foundation and is consistent with the central tenets of the Christian faith.

The main purpose of this paper is to elucidate the foundational compatibility between Christianity and marketing, thus supporting the discipline's suitability as part of a Christian vocation. Unlike other works that have dealt with Christian responses to certain marketing-related ethical issues more superficially, this paper delves deeper into the core of both belief sets, those of marketing and of Christianity, by explicating two intimately related concepts: reconciliation and exchange. In doing so, the paper develops the following important linkage between Christian vocation and marketing: The main purpose of Christian vocation is reconciliation; reconciliation is related inextricably to exchange; exchange is the underlying social behavior that marketing directs; consequently, the proper practice of marketing facilitates mutually beneficial exchange, which fosters reconciliation and thereby supports Christian vocation. In addition, this paper suggests practical ways in which Christians can help to reconcile marketing

---

1   Kathleen Cholewka, "Survey Says: Some Sales Execs are Liars," *Sales & Marketing Management* 153 (February 2001): 18; Richard N. Farmer, "Would You Want Your Son to Marry a Marketing Lady?" *Journal of Marketing* 41 (January 1977): 15-18; Ian Ryder, "Seven Key Challenges for Today's Communicators," *Strategic Communication Management* 7 (December 2002/January 2003): 20-23.

practice to both the discipline's normative theory and to appropriate societal expectations. Given this agenda, it is important to begin with a discussion of the paper's key terms: vocation, reconciliation, marketing, and exchange. I will now treat the first two concepts, vocation and reconciliation, and support how they are intimately related.

Reconciliation: the Main Purpose of Vocation

Much has been written about vocation, and while it is not my intention to review the breadth and depth of literature, I do feel the need to present my own understanding of the concept. Like many others, I see vocation as God's calling for all of one's life. Vocation derives from the Latin verb *vocare*, to call, and from a biblical perspective, that caller is God.[2] It is important to note that this calling applies to every area of one's life, as there is no distinction between sacred and secular.[3] An individual's vocation may include, for instance, his or her role as parent, spouse, sibling, deacon, scout leader, softball player, and choir member. As such, a vocation is a unique, individualized calling, often not discovered easily, that requires specific talents, offers true enjoyment, and accomplishes something of value.[4]

Of course, one's occupation is also part of one's vocation. Here my understanding of vocation is influenced by Lutheran theology, which

---

2   Gary D. Badcock, *The Way of Life* (Grand Rapids, MI: Eerdmans Publishing Co., 1998); Shirley J. Roels, "The Christian Calling to Business Life," *Theology Today* 60 (October 2003): 357-369; Leland Ryken, "Work as stewardship," in *On Moral Business: Classical and Contemporary Resources for Ethics in Economic Life,* ed. Max L. Stackhouse, Dennis P. McCann, and Shirley J. Roels, with Preston N. Williams (Grand Rapids, MI: Eerdmans Publishing Co., 1995): 84-86. *On Moral Business: Classical and Contemporary Resources for Ethics in Economic Life,* eds. Max L. Stackhouse, Dennis P. McCann, and Shirley J. Roels, with Preston N. Williams (Grand Rapids, MI: Eerdmans Publishing Co., 1995).

3   Gary D. Badcock, *The Way of Life* (Grand Rapids, MI: Eerdmans Publishing Co., 1998); Alexander Hill, *Just Business: Christian Ethics for the Marketplace* (Downers Grove, IL: InterVarsity Press, 1997); Arthur F. Holmes, *The Idea of a Christian College* (Grand Rapids, MI: Eerdmans Publishing Co., 1987).

4   Michael Novak, *Business as a Calling: Work and the Examined Life* (New York: The Free Press, 1996), 34-36.

suggests that almost any occupation may be part of a Christian calling.[5] All work has the potential to be of service to God.[6] Because the topic of this paper is "Marketing as a Christian Vocation," the occupational component of vocation is this paper's main focus. It is important to note, however, that marketing is not practiced exclusively as an occupation; marketing may be part of any number of other vocational roles.

Given the preceding description of vocation, one may conclude that every person's vocation is different; God's calling is always unique. Nevertheless, there is a sense that all Christian callings are united by a common purpose. Many see the unifying objective of vocation as loving God and one's neighbors.[7] I agree wholeheartedly with this assertion, which is based soundly on Jesus' greatest commandments.[8] It is every Christian's calling to love God and to love others no matter what his or her specific vocation. I also offer, however, that the desired outcome of this love may be summarized aptly in a single concept: reconciliation. For me, the central purpose of vocation is reconciliation. The works of several Christian scholars, as well as Scripture itself, seem to support this belief that Christian vocation is fundamentally about living a life of reconciliation.

Most Christians are likely to agree that reconciliation is an essential, if not the most fundamental, component of the gospel,[9] but what makes reconciliation integral to vocation? The writings of various scholars help

---

5   Gary D. Badcock, *The Way of Life* (Grand Rapids, MI: Eerdmans Publishing Co., 1998).

6   *Luther's Works: Volume 3, Lectures on Genesis Chapters 15-20*, ed. Jaroslav Pelikan (St. Louis. MO: Concordia Publishing House, 1961), 321; Robert A. Wauzzinaki, "The Gospel, Business, and the State," in *Biblical Principles & Business: The Foundations*, ed. Richard C. Chewning (Colorado Springs, CO: Navpress, 1989), 203-222.

7   Gary D. Badcock, *The Way of Life* (Grand Rapids, MI: Eerdmans Publishing Co., 1998); Douglas J. Schuurman, *Vocation: Discerning Our Callings in Life* (Grand Rapids, MI: Eerdmans Publishing Co., 2004).

8   Matthew 22:36-40.

9   James Denney, *The Christian Doctrine of Reconciliation* (New York: George H. Doran Company, 1918). Charles T. Matthewes, "The Academic Life as a Christian Vocation," *Journal of Religion* 79 (January 1999): 110-121.

to illuminate the important connection. Henlee Barnette contends that because all Christians have themselves been reconciled through Christ, they are called to be agents of reconciliation; she adds, "God calls the Christian with a holy calling and for a definite purpose (Romans 8:28; 9-11; Ephesians 1:11; II Timothy 1:9). His aim for mankind is that of redemption and reconciliation."[10] Douglas Schuurman supports the importance of reconciliation to vocation by maintaining that "the purpose of God's call is for people of God to worship God and to participate in God's creative and redemptive purposes for the world."[11] Gary Badcock suggests that "the Christian calling refers to the reorientation of human life to God through repentance, faith, and obedience."[12] Furthermore, Robert Cushman adds that reconciliation is not restricted to private redemption but includes the restoration of social structures, suggesting that Christian vocation should be seen as "positive engagement with the living Christ in the reconciliation of the whole creation."[13]

The most compelling support for the inseparability of vocation and reconciliation, however, comes from Scripture. As 2 Corinthians 5:18-19 suggests, those who have been reconciled through Christ are called to practice reconciliation: "All this is from God, who reconciled us to himself through Christ and gave us the ministry of reconciliation: that God was reconciling the world to himself in Christ, not counting men's sins against them. And he has committed to us the message of reconciliation." Likewise, Colossians 1:18-20 speaks of Christ as the head of the church and the means through which all things are reconciled to God. It seems reasonable to conclude, then, that Christians, the members of Christ's body, are called to supportive roles in that reconciliation.

---

10   Henlee H. Barnette, *Christian Calling and Vocation* (Grand Rapids, MI: Baker Book House, 1965), 20.

11   Douglas J. Schuurman, *Vocation: Discerning Our Callings in Life* (Grand Rapids, MI: Eerdmans Publishing Co., 2004), 18.

12   Gary D. Badcock, *The Way of Life* (Grand Rapids, MI: Eerdmans Publishing Co., 1998), 9.

13   Robert E. Cushman, *Faith Seeking Understanding: Essays Theological and Critical* (Durham, NC: Duke University Press, 1981), 225-226.

Although the preceding discussion has begun to reveal my understanding of reconciliation, it is appropriate to define this complex construct more completely. My use of the term in this paper stems primarily from the New Testament meanings of three related Greek verbs:[14] *diallasso*: to change; to renew friendship with one;[15] *katallasso*: to change; to exchange for an equivalent value; to return to favor those who are at variance; to adjust a difference;[16] and *apokatallasso*: to bring back to a former state of harmony.[17]

The writings of several Christian scholars help to elucidate the biblical term

further. For instance, in keeping with the idea of returning to a former state of harmony, Badcock suggests, "reconciliation in biblical terms means that we are no longer strangers or enemies [of God] but children and even friends."[18] In terms of a change or an exchange, Cristoph Schwöbel suggests that reconciliation involves exchanging wrath and enmity for love and peace.[19] In addition, although reconciliation should occur first and foremost between an individual and God,[20] this reconciliation with the divine is tied closely to individuals reconciling with each other.[21]

Barnette affirms the preceding point and adds, "The ministry of reconciliation, however, is not limited to bringing men to God, but

---

14 James Strong, *Strong's Greek & Hebrew Dictionary* (Winterbourne, ONT: Online Bible, 1993). William E. Vine, *Vine's Expository Dictionary of Old Testament and New Testament Words* (Nashville, TN: Thomas Nelson, Inc., 1940).

15 Matthew 5:24.

16 Romans 5:10-11; 1 Corinthians 7:11; 2 Corinthians 5:18-20; Colossians 1:21.

17 Ephesians 1:10, 2:16; Colossians 1:20-21; Philippians 2:10.

18 Gary D. Badcock, *The Way of Life* (Grand Rapids, MI: Eerdmans Publishing Co., 1998), 30.

19 Cristoph Schwöbel, "Reconciliation: From Biblical Observations to Dogmatic Reconstruction," in *The Theology of Reconciliation*, ed. Colin E. Gunton (London: T&T Clark Ltd., 2003), 16.

20 James Denney, *The Christian Doctrine of Reconciliation* (New York: George H. Doran Company, 1918).

21 Charles T. Matthewes, "The Academic Life as a Christian Vocation," *Journal of Religion* 79 (January 1999): 110-121.

extends to the reconciliation of men with men. Moreover, all economic, social, and political ideologies are to be captured for Christ."[22] Reconciliation, therefore, is fundamentally about restoring, building, and maintaining strong relationships,[23] and as the following model illustrates, a Christian vocation understood in the broadest sense is one that supports reconciliation between oneself and God, oneself and others, others and God, and others and others.

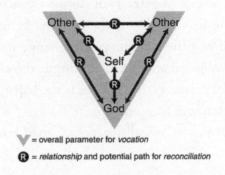

$\blacktriangledown$ = overall parameter for *vocation*

$\textbf{R}$ = *relationship* and potential path for *reconciliation*

FIGURE 1: MODEL OF RECONCILIATION AS VOCATION

I have shared my understanding of two of this paper's main constructs: vocation and reconciliation, arguing that the central purpose of vocation is reconciliation. The main question still remains, however: How can marketing be considered a Christian vocation? Furthermore, by defining vocation in terms of reconciliation, I suggest that marketing must be supportive of reconciliation if the discipline is to be considered a Christian vocation. A key transitional question, therefore, is: How does marketing support reconciliation? In order to address both of these questions, it is important to describe this paper's third and

---

22 Henlee H. Barnette, *Christian Calling and Vocation* (Grand Rapids, MI: Baker Book House, 1965), 20-21.

23 Wayne T. Alderson and Nancy Alderson McDonnell, *Theory R Management* (Nashville, TN: Thomas Nelson, Inc., 1994); Colin E. Gunton, "Towards a Theology of Reconciliation," in *The Theology of Reconciliation,* ed. Colin E. Gunton (London: T&T Clark Ltd., 2003), 167-174.

probably most controversial construct—marketing—as well as the social behavior that marketing is meant to facilitate—exchange.

The American Marketing Association (AMA) describes marketing as "an organizational function and set of processes for creating, communicating and delivering value to customers and for managing customer relationships in ways that benefit the organization and its stakeholders."[24] From this concise yet comprehensive definition of marketing, I would like to extract an implicit concept that many in the field have identified as the core focus of marketing"—exchange.[25] Shelby Hunt confirms the centrality of exchange to marketing as he states, "the basic subject matter of marketing is the exchange relationship or transaction . . . marketing science is the behavioral science that seeks to explain exchange relationships."[26]

Figure 2 provides a visual image of marketing's relationship to exchange.

FIGURE 2: THE CORE FOCUS OF MARKETING

24 The American Marketing Association, "Marketing Definitions," (August 2004) http://www.marketingpower.com /content4620.php (accessed August 9, 2006).

25 Wroe Alderson and Miles W. Martin, "Toward a Formal Theory of Transactions and Transvections," *Journal of Marketing Research* 2 (May 1965): 117-127; Richard P. Bagozzi, "Marketing as Exchange," *Journal of Marketing* 39 (October 1975): 32-39; Philip Kotler, "A Generic Concept of Marketing," *Journal of Marketing* 36 (April 1972): 46-54; Charles W. Lamb, Jr., Joseph F. Hair, Jr., and Carl D. McDaniel, *Marketing*, 7th ed. (Mason, OH: South-Western, 2004).

26 Shelby D. Hunt, *Foundations of Marketing Theory: Toward a General Theory* (Armonk, NY: M.E. Sharpe, 2002), 132.

Marketing seeks to encourage exchange that benefits buyers and sellers equally. Unlike a zero-sum game in which one party must lose in order for the other to win, both parties improve their situations through the exchange.[27] This mutually beneficial exchange begins by sellers first identifying and embracing the needs of buyers[28] and then using that philosophy to guide choices related to: what is exchanged, where and when the exchange takes place, and how buyers and sellers share information related to the exchange. In doing so, marketing strives to maximize the value of the exchange, or the ratio of benefits received to costs incurred.[29] The central purpose of marketing, therefore, is to facilitate valuable, or mutually beneficial, exchange.

The next logical question, then, is: How does exchange, the central focus of marketing, support reconciliation? Exchange is a fundamental human behavior that involves two or more parties each receiving something of value by offering something of value in return. The parties participate in the transaction voluntarily because all expect to be better off as a result.[30] God established exchange as part of the created order.[31] Even before the Fall, Adam and Eve offered their work and care for the Garden in exchange for its fruits. God also made humans with different talents and abilities, thereby necessitating that individuals and groups exchange with each other in order to lead productive lives. For

---

27 George S. Day, *Strategic Market Planning: The Pursuit of Competitive Advantage* (St. Paul, MN: West Publishing Company, 1984).

28 George S. Day, "The Capabilities of Market-Driven Organizations," *Journal of Marketing* 58 (October 1994): 37-52; Ajay K. Kohli and Bernard J. Jaworski, "Market Orientation: The Construct, Research Propositions, and Managerial Implications," *Journal of Marketing* 54 (April 1990): 1-18; Philip Kotler and Gary Armstrong, *Principles of Marketing*, 8th ed. (Upper Saddle River, NJ: Prentice-Hall, Inc., 1999). Philip Kotler and Sidney J. Levy, "Broadening the Concept of Marketing," *Journal of Marketing* 33 (January 1969): 10-15.

29 Charles W. Lamb, Jr., Joseph F. Hair, Jr., and Carl D. McDaniel, *Marketing,* 7th ed. (Mason, OH: South-Western, 2004).

30 Philip Kotler, *Marketing Management: The Millennium Edition* (Upper Saddle River, NJ: Prentice-Hall, Inc., 2000).

31 Roels, "The Christian Calling to Business Life," *Theology Today* 60 (October 2003), 359.

example, 1 Kings 5 recounts how Solomon and Hiram, King of Tyre, cooperated in exchanging their nations' resources in order to build the temple in Jerusalem. Likewise, the body of Christ, with its many different parts, serving a variety of complementary functions, seems to be an entity designed for exchange.[32]

Just as the need to exchange serves as a means for bringing individuals and groups into positive relationships, ongoing mutually beneficial exchange seems to be associated with the maintenance of strong interpersonal rapport. When parties are estranged, or not reconciled, they tend to avoid exchange. When spouses become alienated, they often fail to exchange words and affections. When nations become estranged, one of the first reactions is to curtail trade and diplomatic discourse. When buyers and sellers have disputes, products are seldom sold or purchased. "Confrontation demeans, destroys, and diminishes. Reconciliation results in growth, dignity, and mutual benefit to both parties."[33] In reconciled states there tends to be free-flowing, mutually beneficial exchange.

At a minimum, the phenomenon of exchange appears to be consistent with the concept of reconciliation. It also seems likely, based on the preceding examples, that exchange is a key ingredient of reconciliation and that reconciliation promotes exchange. Furthermore, one might even argue that reconciliation is exchange when one considers, as mentioned earlier, that the Greek New Testament meaning of reconciliation involves changing something relatively undesirable for something desirable, establishing a favorable state, and achieving value for all participants. So, by facilitating mutually beneficial exchange, marketing supports a God-given behavior that is consistent with, if not instrumental to, reconciliation. Presuming that the central purpose of vocation is reconciliation, the core of marketing appears uniquely

---

32   1 Corinthians 12:12-31.

33   Wayne T. Alderson and Nancy Alderson McDonnell, *Theory R Management* (Nashville, TN: Thomas Nelson, Inc., 1994), xv.

suited to serve as part of a Christian calling. It is important to note that the preceding discussion describes what marketing should be ideally. This paper's next section compares this normative description to actual marketing practice, both good and bad.

Reconciling Misconceptions of Marketing

Given the inherent consistency between marketing and Christian vocation, why do so many people still believe, as this paper's introduction has suggested, that the discipline fosters estrangement, not reconciliation? Unfortunately, such attitudes toward marketing are not entirely unfounded. The blame, however, does not rest with the fundamental tenets of the discipline but with the actions that some people and organizations take under the auspices of marketing. Every day, marketers facilitate a variety of exchanges that benefit buyers and sellers equally. For example, to a great extent, marketing is the reason why consumers don't have to drive to Battle Creek, MI to buy their breakfast cereal; a congregation is aware of its church's upcoming Worship Arts Weekend; bread costs $2.50 a loaf, not $5.00; and people can see well despite poor vision.

Regrettably, however, some sellers, under the guise of marketing, promote exchanges that favor themselves disproportionately. It is reasonable to conclude that these types of exchanges encourage dissonance rather than reconciliation. It is also important to note, however, that this category of actions does not reflect the core purpose of marketing accurately, as previously developed.

In order to address the discipline's apparent inconsistencies, it is helpful to distinguish inappropriate marketing practice from a proper conceptualization of the discipline. Such an aim is consistent with the work of Shelby Hunt, who differentiates positive marketing theory (actual observed marketing behavior) from normative knowledge of the discipline (what marketing strategy should be). Hunt further delineates two types of normative knowledge: rational normative, which is based on marketing's fundamental tenets, and ethical normative, which stems from moral principles.[34] The following section seeks to strengthen the argument further that marketing supports reconciliation and, therefore, can be part of a Christian vocation by analyzing the positive and normative dimensions of three common marketing misconceptions in light of the preceding framework.

First Misconception:
Marketing Theory Encourages Selling Things to People That They Do Not Need

One of the most common indictments of marketing theory is that it supports selling products to people that they do not need. Of course, at the root of this issue is the question of what constitutes a need. In the strictest sense, people need very few things to survive: air, water, food, clothing, shelter. The point, however, is not to argue that marketing is constrained by too narrow a definition of "need." One can concede that people need things beyond basic elements of survival; for example, people may need cars for transportation or need phones for communication, yet some products still seem to exceed the limits of what represents reasonable consumption. For instance, in a recent catalog, toy retailer F.A.O. Schwartz offered a $15,000 child-size Mercedes with rack-and-pinion steering and a $30,000 playhouse with bay windows.

Most people hear of these items and conclude quickly that there is no legitimate need for such products. I tend to agree with this judgment and add that ultimately such exchanges foster estrangement, not reconciliation. Although many kids would be thrilled to take ownership of a $30,000 playhouse, discord is likely to occur as parents rationalize the extreme gift as a reason for spending less time with their children, as envious friends become disenchanted with their own more

---

34 Shelby D. Hunt, *Foundations of Marketing Theory: Toward a General Theory* (Armonk, NY: M.E. Sharpe, 2002).

modest toys, and as the young playhouse recipients develop a distorted view of money and possessions.

Likewise I will argue, however, that rational normative marketing knowledge also rejects the sale of such products. Although these exchanges may appear first to be mutually beneficial, they really are not. The probable outcomes described above and others like them (for example, children begin to lose interest in the playhouse after a few weeks) suggest that a family will never realize $30,000 worth of benefits from the purchase. The notion that the exchange is really not mutually beneficial should be reason enough to dissuade a marketer from promoting such a transaction, even if actual marketing practice sometimes suggests otherwise.

When practiced in a way that is consistent with its core tenets, marketing never seeks to sell things to consumers that they do not need but rather supports exchanges that produce real value for buyers and sellers. As such, marketing facilitates a virtually limitless number of valuable exchanges, helping to meet needs that vary from employment to entertainment, from food to friendship, and from education to esteem. As developed earlier, these exchanges themselves may play a role in reconciliation. Furthermore, having lower-level needs met may allow people to fulfill higher-level needs[35] and, perhaps, other forms of reconciliation.

Second Misconception:
Marketing Theory Supports Deception in order to Get People to Buy Products

A second common criticism of marketing theory is that it advocates using deception to persuade people to buy products. This criticism is perhaps levied most often at advertising, marketing's primary form of mass communication. First, it is important to understand that advertising is advocacy, and advertisers have a right to put their best foot

---

35   Abraham H. Maslow, "A Theory of Human Motivation," *Psychological Review* 50 (July 1943): 370-396.

forward, or to present their products in a favorable light.[36] Consumers are justified, however, in bemoaning television commercials that suggest an SUV can climb an unrealistically steep and treacherous hill, or magazine ads whose models' glistening white teeth are due more to photo retouching than use of the advertised dental product. It is truly regrettable that there are instances of deception in some marketing promotion, for these types of practices certainly do not foster reconciliation. On the contrary, deceptive marketing communication is likely to stir resentment among buyers[37] who will terminate the exchange relationships when the deception is discovered. Unfortunately, such deception might also lead to estrangement in other relationships. For instance, family members may resent the purchaser for "wasting money," or consumers might grow to distrust marketers in general.

The practice of deceptive communication does not constitute the majority of positive marketing practice, however, nor does it represent normative marketing knowledge, the reasons for which are very similar to those outlined in the previous section. As inferred earlier, consumers who realize they have been deceived are unlikely to be satisfied with the exchange in question and, when possible, will try to avoid further association with that particular seller, and sometimes with that entire category of sellers. Deceptive communication is, therefore, antithetical to marketing's goals of facilitating mutually beneficial exchange and forging positive long-term relationships.

In contrast, when marketing communication is practiced with integrity, as it often is, buyers and sellers benefit and reconciliation is supported. For example, there are tens of thousands of ads that inform consumers realistically and accurately of potential exchanges such as ones involving sales of breakfast cereals, releases of newly published

---

36 Edward D. Zinbarg, *Faith, Morals, and Money: What the World's Religions tell us about Ethics in the Marketplace* (New York: The Continuum International Publishing Group Inc., 2001).

37 Douglas J. Schuurman, *Vocation: Discerning Our Callings in Life* (Grand Rapids, MI: Eerdmans Publishing Co., 2004).

books, and meetings of single parent support groups. Honest marketing communication, therefore, directly and indirectly supports positive relationships, or states of favor, among a variety of different parties. Such marketing facilitates exchange and reconciliation.

Third Misconception:

Marketing Theory Suggests that a Given Product should be Sold to Everyone

A third and final misunderstanding of marketing theory is that it encourages sellers to try to persuade all consumers to adopt their product offerings. It is true that sellers can potentially increase their own rewards by benefiting a greater number of buyers, and corporations often are under pressure to grow, which may mean expanding their markets and reaching more consumers. Unfortunately, there are instances of sellers trying to push their products outside a reasonable circle of consumers. For example, many people have received direct mail pieces that seemed entirely misdirected, such as a couple renting an apartment receives a mailing for new vinyl replacement windows, or a single, middle-age man receives a postcard announcing a sale at a teen girls' clothing store.

These examples seem rather benign, yet it would be difficult to argue that they support reconciliation, and other more intrusive promotions may actually provoke estrangement. For instance, the national Do-Not-Call List appears to reflect many consumers' disdain for the telemarketing of products that are often irrelevant to the consumers' needs. These types of examples do, unfortunately, represent actual marketing behavior to some extent. Such practices do not, however, represent the discipline's normative knowledge, or what marketing strategy should be.

In marketing, the quantity of prospective consumers should be secondary to the qualities of the consumers. The main reason that quality supersedes quantity is that not all buyers want or need the same things, and marketing is predicated upon creating beneficial exchanges, or meeting people's needs. In the aggregate, consumer demand tends to be divergent and heterogeneous,[38] which should lead a marketer to segment the whole market into smaller groups of more homogenous buyers who do have similar needs[39] and to target only that group of consumers whose needs the marketer is best suited to meet.[40] In addition, qualities of consumers are important because marketing theory values people and relationships,[41] a focus that encourages marketers to demonstrate care and compassion in their exchanges.

These market segmentation and target marketing strategies offer benefits both to buyers and sellers. First, by targeting a smaller and more homogenous group of consumers, organizations are able to satisfy those consumers' preferences more precisely and effectively.[42] Such need fulfillment is, of course, appealing to consumers. Second, organizations benefit by being able to make more efficient use of their limited resources, which enhances their profitability.[43] It is unreasonable for sellers to try to sell to all potential buyers, and it is impractical for firms to try to bring about a convergence of divergent consumer demand.[44]

---

38   Wendell R. Smith, "Product Differentiation and Market Segmentation as Alternative Marketing Strategies," *Journal of Marketing* 21 (July 1956): 3-8.

39   Theodore Levitt, *The Marketing Imagination* (New York: The Free Press, 1986).

40   George S. Day, *Strategic Market Planning: The Pursuit of Competitive Advantage* (St. Paul, MN: West Publishing Company, 1984).

41   Martin Christopher, Adrian Payne, and David Ballantyne, *Relationship Marketing: Bringing Quality, Customer Service, and Marketing Together* (Oxford, England: Butterworth-Heinemann Ltd., 1993); Jonathan R. Copulsky and Michael J. Wolf, "Relationship Marketing: Positioning for the Future," *Journal of Business Strategy* 11 (July/August 1990): 16-20; Christian Grönroos, "Quo Vadis, Marketing? Toward a Relationship Marketing Paradigm," *Journal of Marketing Management* 10 (July 1994): 347-360; Michael D. Johnson and Fred Selnes "Customer Portfolio Management: Toward a Dynamic Theory of Exchange Relationships," *Journal of Marketing* 68 (April 2004): 1-17.

42   Wendell R. Smith, "Product Differentiation and Market Segmentation as Alternative Marketing Strategies," *Journal of Marketing* 21 (July 1956): 3-8.

43   Yoram Wind, "Issues and Advances in Segmentation Research," *Journal of Marketing Research* 15 (August 1978): 317-337.

44   Wendell R. Smith, "Product Differentiation and Market Segmentation as Alternative Marketing Strategies," *Journal of Marketing* 21 (July 1956): 3-8.

When market segmentation and target marketing are employed, reconciliation is supported again. Consumers tend not to become disgruntled with marketers because consumers receive promotional messages for items in which they are interested. For example, a 30-year-old mother reading Good Housekeeping sees an ad for a vehicle with special child safety features, or a teenager listening to Christian radio hears an ad announcing the release of one of her favorite artist's new CDs. In such instances, marketing directly cultivates positive relationships between buyers and sellers. Furthermore, to the extent that marketing helps to fulfill some of consumers' basic needs, the discipline also enables people to move to higher-level need fulfillment, including that of other social needs.[45] Such marketing facilitates exchange and reconciliation.

Implications: The Roles of Christians in Reconciling Marketing

Having developed and supported the legitimacy of marketing's claim to Christian vocation, there remains the practical question of how the day-to-day practice of marketing can be reconciled both to the field's normative theory and to proper societal expectations of the discipline. More specifically, given this article's focus and the readership of *Christian Scholar's Review*, an even more relevant question considers the role that believers might play in redeeming, or reclaiming, the marketing function. There is, of course, no simple prescription for resolving the deep-rooted and longstanding tensions surrounding marketing. In order to move toward reconciliation, it is important that attitudes toward the discipline change for both marketers and consumers, given that exchange is a social phenomenon that involves two or more parties. To that end, the following paragraphs outline how three main groups of Christian stakeholders can encourage marketing's reconciliation.

---

45   Abraham H. Maslow, "A Theory of Human Motivation," *Psychological Review* 50 (July 1943): 370-396.

Christian Higher Education

Perhaps the most obvious place to start with recommendations for change is within Christian colleges and universities, where a large number of future leaders in business and other fields develop long-lasting attitudes toward the discipline. Business faculty should take the lead, first in debunking the belief that marketing is simply advertising and selling, a notion that unnecessarily relegates the discipline to a narrow promotional role. Instead, Christian-business educators must help their own students, as well as students and faculty from other disciplines, learn about the true nature, or full scope, of marketing; that is, that marketing involves optimizing decisions related to products, distribution, pricing, and communication in order to best meet consumers' needs, thereby creating mutually beneficial exchange. Likewise, business faculty should help consumers across campus recognize and appreciate how marketing activities make possible the products and services upon which everyone depends daily, for example, food, clothing, and transportation. This education must, of course, start in the classroom, but should then extend into other venues that reach more interdisciplinary audiences, such as public lectures, alternative chapels, seminars, panel discussions, collaborative research, and service projects.

The Church

As implied earlier, the Church is at times not an especially friendly environment for businesspeople, meaning that marketers, in particular, can be made to feel that their discipline undermines biblical teaching and Christian values. Some of this perceived conflict stems from the same narrow stereotyping of marketing described above, which can be addressed in similar ways. Beyond these measures, it is important for pastors and other Church leaders to affirm the legitimate and helpful roles of marketers and other Christian businesspeople within their congregations. This movement toward broader acceptance might begin by recognizing the precedent for "biblical businesspeople," for example, Job (a livestock magnate; Job 1:3), Lydia (a textile merchant; Acts 16:14), and Jesus (a carpenter/tradesman; Mark 6:3). Successful Christian businesspeople also should be encouraged to excel in the "grace of giving" (2 Corinthians 8:7), a spiritual gift that many possess, which can assist the Church's ministries greatly. In addition, the Church should appreciate the potential that marketers and other Christian businesspeople have to utilize their discipline-specific skills to further the Church's mission. For instance, many churches can use help in researching community needs, branding new programs, and promoting unique ministries.

Christians in Business/Marketing

The third group of stakeholders consists of Christian marketers themselves. The main way that these individuals can help to reconcile the discipline is by practicing it according to the normative theory described throughout this paper. Positive examples of mutually beneficial exchange will speak volumes more than any verbal defense of the discipline. In addition, it is helpful to reiterate one specific biblical guideline that lies at the heart of reconciliation—the Golden Rule: Treat others the way that you want to be treated, or as Jesus said, "Love your neighbor as yourself" (Mark 12:31). In following this one principle, Christian marketers will also uphold several other important mandates effectively, for instance, thinking long-term, considering all parties affected by one's actions, and putting people ahead of things. Ultimately, such a focus will produce the mutually beneficial exchange and reconciliation this entire paper has sought.

Concluding Thoughts

To summarize, I have argued that reconciliation is the central purpose of Christian vocation; therefore, an occupation or discipline must support reconciliation in order to be part of a Christian calling. Furthermore,

I have attempted to establish that marketing, through its facilitation of mutually beneficial exchanges, is consistent with and supportive of reconciliation. Consequently, I have maintained that marketing can be part of a Christian vocation.

I would like to add that the discussion of whether marketing can be a Christian calling is vitally important not just for Christians who work or intend to work in marketing, but for everyone. The basis for this sweeping claim is that marketing involves and affects everyone. Although relatively few people practice marketing as an occupation, virtually everyone is a marketer of something. While individuals may not market products in the commercial sense, they do market their personal services and ideas. In addition, every living person participates in exchanges from a consumer's perspective.[46]

Furthermore, marketing has a tremendous impact on our world's social and economic structures. Many believe that business is the world's most dominant institution,[47] and marketing, which is at the heart of commerce, may be the quintessential business discipline. The power and influence of marketing is immense. Many of the world's largest corporations generate revenues of more than $200 billion a year and employ hundreds of thousands of people in the process of exchanging their products and services. While some might view this influence with dismay, a more enlightened perspective envisions the potential that marketing has to help overcome many societal woes.[48] When understood and practiced as part of a Christian vocation, marketing directs the God-given phenomenon of exchange rightly, affording a

---

46 Kenneth S. Kantzer, "God Intends His Precepts to Transform Society," in *Biblical Principles & Business: The Foundations,* ed. Richard C. Chewning (Colorado Springs, CO: Navpress, 1989), 22-34.

47 William H. Shaw and Vincent Barry, *Moral Issues in Business,* 10th ed. (Belmont, CA: Thomson Wadsworth, 2007); *On Moral Business: Classical and Contemporary Resources for Ethics in Economic Life,* eds. Max L. Stackhouse, Dennis P. McCann, and Shirley J. Roels, with Preston N. Williams (Grand Rapids, MI: Eerdmans Publishing Co., 1995).

48 Michael Novak, *Business as a Calling: Work and the Examined Life* (New York: The Free Press, 1996), 37; Shirley J. Roels, "The Christian Calling to Business Life," *Theology Today* 60 (October 2003): 357-369.

unique opportunity to support reconciliation in our world. Christian higher education should be a leader in encouraging individuals to practice marketing as part of their divine calling.

CPSIA information can be obtained
at www.ICGtesting.com
Printed in the USA
BVOW08s2301220118
505499BV00001B/110/P